The Bunny Hugging Terrorist

Joan Court

With a Preface by Tony Benn

SELENE PRESS

Published by Selene Press
74 Sturton Street
Cambridge
CB1 2QA
Tel: 01223 311828

ISBN 0-9543452-0-5

British Library Cataloguing in Publication Data
A CIP catalogue record for this book is available from the British Library

Cover Design by Yvone Pollock

Printed by Elitian Ltd, 112 Mill Road, Cambridge CB1 2BD

Foreword

In this book, Joan Court brings a natural tenderness, burning anger and intellectual curiosity to bear on the wickedness that is perpetrated by humans against animals, whether it be in the abattoir, the medical laboratory or in the name of conservation.

When I was a child, my family used to walk out on Sundays to Trafalgar Square and just opposite the Whitehall Theatre, there was a shop run by the Anti-Vivisectionist League. On display in the window were several stuffed animals being tortured, supposedly for medical research. I used to stop and look with a horror that still remains.

Then in the early 1980's my son Hilary said: "Dad, if the world ate the grain instead of feeding it to cattle and eating the meat, there would be enough food for everyone", and in that one moment he converted his parents to vegetarianism.

Since then I have become a firm supporter of the animal rights movement, to which Joan Court has dedicated the latter part of her life. Her career path has been fascinating, first as a midwife, later as a social worker and expert on child abuse, and then as a "mature student" in Cambridge where she discovered the "research" that was being carried out and began the campaign for which she is best known. In this book her intelligence, passion and humour light up every page.

Now 90, she is a shining example of grey power and the effectiveness of resistance to the established order of things. The animal rights movement is the anti slavery campaign of the 21st century and it will succeed.

Tony Benn
April 2009

For Donna Bull

and

In memory of Hilda Ruse

Also by the same author

In the Shadow of Mahatma Gandhi

Selene Press

Acknowledgements

This book is dedicated to Donna Bull, whose unfailing encouragement and patient revision of the text has been invaluable.

I am grateful to my spiritual sister, Nicola Carmichael, whose hospitality enabled me to write without distractions. Also to Vanessa Clarke and Dr Glenn Lyons who edited the book; David Jarvis who patiently transferred the handwritten manuscript onto his computer; Joni Metcalf who first tried to work from my tapes but had to give up because of my ineptitude with gadgets; Fiona Jones for her careful proof reading and support and to Yvone Pollock who designed the book cover. Finally, to my fictive great grand-daughter, Roz, seventy years younger than me who, when I told her that I didn't know where I stood on so many animal rights issues, said "perhaps you'll find out when you write".

My friends and fellow warriors in the animal rights movement have been both an inspiration and an inhibitor because I cannot do justice to them. They include Fiona, Fran, Aran, Sheila, Pat, Sue, Greta, Eloise, Ellie- Jo, Greta, Ros, Tony Vernelli, Tony Rolls, the Rev James Thompson, Vanessa, Angela, Robert, Amanda's (all three), my five fictive brothers and......

Those of us in the Animal Rights Movement owe a debt, usually unacknowledged, to the campaigning national movements, especially to Animal Aid and it's brilliant Director, Andrew Tyler; to Viva! led by Juliet Gellatley and to Tony Wardle who pioneered a new revolutionary approach in exposing the nightmare imposed on animals in factory farms and slaughter houses. And my respect and admiration for the team who monitor and campaign against live export, and to Carla Lane who stays with it and uses her expertise and celebrity status in Europe.

Above all, my love and gratitude to my friends who are imprisoned, awaiting trial or who have been severely injured for their total dedication to the animal rights movement and in memory of those who have died violently while seeking to save the lives of animals.

We all owe a great debt to under cover workers who have bravely obtained first hand evidence of the cruelty and degrading practices in laboratories, factory farms and circuses.

The comradeship of my friends in the movement binds us in love and sorrow and is the greatest solace and spur to keep going, and personally inspired me to write this book.

Joan Court
April 2009

Contents

APPENDICES

"Cowardice asks the question is it safe?

Expediency asks the question is it politic?

But conscience asks the question is it right?

And there comes a time when one must take a position that is neither safe nor politic, nor popular, but because conscience tells one it is right."

Martin Luther King

Joan and Maisie

Introduction

Animal liberation is the abolitionist movement for the twenty-first century and it is inextricably linked with human liberation and saving our planet. History has taught us that we must not only speak out against injustice but we must act out against it using all our power and strength. Change only comes when concerned citizens cause enough of a ruckus that the apathetic majority are forced to take notice.

Tony Vernelli

This book is a sequel to *In the Shadow of Mahatma Gandhi* in which I described my earlier life and my thirst for education and adventure. The other strand is the strength of my feelings about the abuse of power and the exploitation of those who do not have a voice or are overwhelmed by circumstances. I was influenced by the novels of Elizabeth Gaskell and Charles Dickens, who described the state of working class people in the nineteenth century and the tales of the workhouse.

I trained as a nurse midwife and in 1947, supported by the Quakers, worked in the slums of Calcutta, then joining the Frontier Nursing Service to work with poverty-stricken families in Kentucky where the nurses rode on horseback to their clients. Much later, I retrained to be a social worker and was initially employed by the NSPCC. After they dismissed me for questioning the power structure, I worked in central government advising on child abuse, and then as a child protection officer. My own all too common personal experience of family neglect and violence meant that I could draw on this experience to understand the child's situation, many of whom are caught in a web of deceit, guilt and pity, a vortex of misery and confusion.

Moving from London to Cambridge in 1977 to read for a degree, I became aware of the terrible suffering of animals in local laboratories. I have always passionately loved animals and felt a great empathy for them, but I had no idea of the scale of individual and institutional suffering they experienced at the hands of tormentors in laboratories, factory farms, the live export trade, zoos, circuses, and every situation where greed and indifference make their lives a living hell.

As Jeff Masson commented in an interview (*Archangel,* Issue 31), "the world as we perceive it is a deeply flawed one... most people manage to avoid seeing it... I sometimes feel I have no place in the world. Of course the fact that millions of other people feel the same way as I do is a great comfort. We are not alone."

The animal rights movement, as Toni Vernelli comments, is the greatest social movement of the century. It is world wide and people are beginning to understand that animals have complex feelings and varied intelligence, and we abuse them at our peril. To harm other sentient beings is spiritually harmful and I do not believe that those engaged in vivisection, factory farming or fishing can be other than desensitised, cruel and totally oblivious to the suffering they cause in the name of science or the production of meat or fish. We cannot stand back and witness cruelty to animals any more than our forebears who worked for the abolition of slavery and other blatant injustices such as apartheid and torture. Appalling suffering is endured by humans all over the world, but compassion is not limited and late in life I chose to be an animal advocate. Unlike other campaigns, the animal rights movement focuses on the suffering of other species, creatures who cannot organise themselves to resist their tormentors and so are totally at their mercy.

It is hard to cope with the anger and sadness that beset us, but we feel impelled to act. Individuals choose different paths. Some are militant, risking imprisonment by deliberately breaking the law. Although I am imprinted with the philosophy of Gandhi and Martin Luther King and others who believe that change can be achieved through non-violence, I recognise that we have a multi-faceted campaign that includes direct action, civil disobedience and education. In fact, many of us have an investment in all these tactics to achieve animal liberation. I am impatient and emotional by nature. People are often criticised for being emotional but it seems to me to be a quite proper response in the circumstances.

I am proud to be in the movement and feel privileged to know so many valiant and loving campaigners who are ready to give up their freedom and risk major disruption to their families, careers, peace of mind and health in order to save animals. Welfare in regard to animals is not enough, though it has its place. What we aim for is a complete change of attitudes, a spiritual awakening that condemns cruelty, sadism and exploitation of animals in all its forms. Incremental improvements have their place, and the public salve their conscience buying free-range eggs and organic milk or other products, but I am drawn to a more revolutionary approach and not to half measures which do little to undermine or overthrow the systems that condemn sentient beings to a lifetime of agony and frustration. In our defence of animal rights, we meet with increasing state oppression which influences the media so we have been described as terrorists - a ridiculous misuse of the word. We fight for justice in the knowledge that change is always possible and that we are impelled to resist tyranny in whatever form it takes.

Chapter 1

New Hall

"Innumerable are sentient beings, we vow to save them all!"

Bodhisattva

Mike held the frog in his hand, removing it carefully from his plastic lunchbox. I took it immediately to put it in the pond, as frogs suffer if they are kept in a warm hand. It disappeared under a lily. "I must get back to school,' said Mike, 'or they'll miss me. I got it from the lab. I don't want him dissected. Seeya!'

Mike returned in a few days, with his mate, carrying a large black rabbit, whom we called Augustus, and his smaller rabbit friend Colette. 'We took them from a nasty home', said Mike, and I made no further enquiries. It is a small consolation to give a home to persecuted creatures.

I was not really involved in animal rights until I came to Cambridge, though I loved cats with an excessive devotion, possibly because of Simpson, the little cat that saved my reason when I was three years old. My brother Peter was born in 1917 into a well-to-do professional family and I followed two years later. My father, a solicitor, committed suicide while we were still very young. My mother was an alcoholic. Simpson was my purring playmate during the long and lonely days when my mother was out drinking, and it was Simpson who cuddled in bed with me, warm and singing gently when my mother returned home after dark, raging and raving. And so cats have always padded through my life.

In the mid-1960s, while I was working in Turkey with the World Health Organisation, I had a tree full of feral cats outside my office window. I fed them by throwing eggs and bread through the window as I could not get into the enclosed garden and they adjusted well to the routine of flying food. In Calcutta in 1945 I did my best for the stray cats who scavenged the rubbish heaps along with Bustee children and wandering cows. In Pakistan in the early 1950s I had inherited Simon, a seal-point Siamese and UN refugee who was passed from family to family as workers finished their contracts, like a letter lost in the post. He returned to England with me in 1955, survived quarantine and helped to keep me sane as I made the difficult transition from my long career as a nurse midwife to graduating in social work in 1957.

For the next 20 years I worked for abused children, pioneering a project on Battered Child Syndrome (as it was then called) for the NSPCC, until the enraged director fired me for questioning an aspect of their policy. I suspected I 'wanted out' in any case. A long psychoanalysis has made me aware of the complexity of my own motives and feelings. My rather sudden departure from the NSPCC in about 1972 was followed by five rather boring years as a civil servant, working in central government for the DHSS as a professional social work advisor on child abuse. I was a very inept civil servant, but as a recognised expert on child abuse I had the knowledge needed at that time to further the cause of child protection. Quite often I was asked to work as an expert witness in court cases involving a child's death or severe injury. Recent medical advances are now bringing to light cases where parents have been apparently wrongly accused of causing cot death or injury to their infants. I only hope the pendulum has not swung too far in the parents' favour because if we deny that babies and young children can on occasion be harmed by their parents they will lose the little protection they now enjoy.

My five years in the civil service ended in 1977 when I was 60 – then retirement age. I moved from London to Cambridge, where through some miraculous coincidences[1] I had been accepted to read for a degree in Social Anthropology at New Hall. I had Pushkin, my little Siamese, in her basket, but my matronly tortoiseshell, Suki-Susanna-Victoria-Puss-in-Boots, stayed in London for a time and joined me later when I had a flat.

---

[1]   See *In the Shadow of Mahatma Gandhi*, published 2004.

As I left school when I was twelve years old, I have ever since yearned for education, which makes me deeply sympathetic to children in developing nations struggling so valiantly to get to school. This hunger of the mind may be lost in most of our own schools, driven out by boredom, exams, and so-called modules, bringing death to imagination and creativity. But this was not the case in the University of Cambridge where you were left, more or less, to find your own way.

Term started at New Hall in October 1977 and we were briefly interviewed by our future tutor who looked after our welfare. Sitting on the floor outside her office, I met another London-based student, Nicola – half my age, as most of my friends are –but over the years she has become my beloved spiritual sister. I was studying Social Anthropology on a two-year course as my previous MA from America enabled me to miss the first year. This was a pity. I would have liked to read Archaeology, which was taught in the first year and would have opened up yet another world to me.

At Cambridge it was not compulsory to go to lectures but, needless to say, I went to every one. I was immersed in the magical world of the Trobriand Islands in New Guinea, and enthralled by our study of Amazon tribal people, learning the complex structures of lineage, all highly theoretical and heady stuff, and for me an amazing change from the language of social work, psycho-dynamics and casework. The societies we studied, particularly in Africa, have largely been annihilated in the last decade or two by war and famine and the breakdown of social structures. I doubt whether the totems and symbols of the Nuer have survived, nor their beautiful horned cattle, nor the elaborate exchange system and magic of the Trobriand islanders. I suspect they are now watching television rather than engaging in a complex social exchange of bracelets and white shells.

I am sure it is good for the mind and soul to be plunged into a new dimension like this. Even now, at 89, I constantly dream of embarking on another degree, for instance, going back to Smith College, Massachusetts, to read for a PhD in that highly intense atmosphere, so very different from the University of Cambridge which by comparison was highly intellectual and cold. Not only cold emotionally, but bitterly cold as the winds rushed in from Siberia over the bleak East Anglian landscape. But the course was enthralling, as I struggled with matrilineal kinship, which I found particularly difficult as I have little personal concept or experience of family life and find it difficult to understand the complexities of family relationships.

During the course, we free-ranged over a vast field of knowledge; providing food for the imagination. As I had never learnt how to study systematically and there were no modules to contain me, I swept across the board of learning. I was required to hand in an essay each week, and this I did adequately, though my supervisor kindly advised me to keep away from Marx, whom she assumed, quite rightly, would be beyond my intellectual capacity. I was always an extremely neurotically anxious student, given to telephoning the Samaritans during an essay crisis. When I rang a friend in London once, I was strangely reassured when she told me, "Things can only get worse". Even so, I still felt that I had landed in Paradise.

Riding home on my bike late one night, the full moon lighting up King's College, I mused that if I could pass my bloody Tripos I could stay in this enchanted city forever. And 27 years later I still feel the same way, despite the dark shadows that emerged as I learned of the cruel and mindless programme of vivisection conducted in Cambridge laboratories.

It was an amazing two years, though sometimes very lonely, particularly after leaving so much of my social life in London. I didn't mix much with other students (apart from Nicola) as I assumed the age barrier would inhibit any friendship. Things have changed now, with a greater influx of mature students. But as a romantic I loved Cambridge. Both Nicola and I graduated and after the ceremony we went off to Midsummer Common, still with our gowns on, and had a riotous time on the dodgems and roundabouts.

Chapter Two

Graduation

Love the animals. God has given them the rudiments of thought and untroubled joy. Do not therefore trouble them, do not torture them, do not deprive them of their joy.

Dostoyevsky: The Brothers Karamazov

I was sixty when I graduated from New Hall in 1979 with my degree in Social Anthropology and I swapped my student card for an old age pension book. I was by then established in my own home in Cambridge with Pushkin and Suki, both of whom had comforted me when I moved to Cambridge as a student.

Restless for a time, I was unsure what to do next. I knew I wanted to go back to India and that if I was going to work there I needed to update my midwifery skills, so I did a refresher course locally and got back on to the Midwifery Roll. I remembered the advice of Dame Eileen Younghusband, social work doyenne and my mentor during the turbulent years I worked for the NSPCC pioneering work on child abuse. I had been fired by the NSPCC for questioning their authority, and was subsequently 'recruited' by central government as an adviser on child abuse, at that time called "battered baby syndrome". When I had told Dame Eileen of my plan to read a degree in Social Anthropology, she had said to me 'And then you can go back to India, find a tribe and do a research degree'. So leaving my beloved soul sister Nicola to care for the house and the cats, I set off for Bengal.

Bela, a dear friend who had shared my life and work when we were pioneering maternal and child welfare in India in 1945, met me at Howrah station in Calcutta. Struggling over leaking boxes of fish on the platform, slipping and sliding and clutching our bedding rolls and suitcases, we pushed our way through the crowds, heading for Bhubareswar in Orissa, where Bela worked with the Kasturba Gandhi Memorial Trust in a remote village orphanage caring for Satyabhama tribal children. As ever, I was happy to be with her in simple, quiet surroundings. The centre was surrounded by luxurious coconut trees and by plants and bushes so covered with butterflies the blossoms were invisible. The loving children gathered around me at the end of the day, anxious to practise their English and teach me their songs and I helped them with their homework.

The days passed quietly, though on one occasion as I was going for my shower, which consisted of pouring water from a clay vessel, I noticed a rather large snake coming up through the drainage hole. It was probably perfectly harmless and only coming up to get cool, but as snakes frequently killed the local villagers there was panic. Sadly, the snake was killed.

Bela had some days off and had contacted a local anthropologist who had worked among the tribal hill people in Orissa, who said he would be happy to tell me of his work and to help me find a possible venue for a field study with tribal people.

In this eastern forested mountain area, home of Mowgli, consisting of the states of Jharkhand, Orissa, and Chhattisgarh, the villages were then untouched. Ninety million tribal people lived in this area, descendants of those who lived here long before the great Aryan invasion. But the land is rich in mineral resources and contains more than 50% of India's mineral wealth. Coal, gold, uranium and iron ore are now being ruthlessly exploited, bringing unmitigated disaster to the tribal people. As the bulldozers and excavations storm into isolated villages, local people who offer resistance have been shot by heavily armed police. But there is now some support for the Naxalites – Maoists named after a West Bengali town who are swarming into India after their successes in Nepal, armed with modern weapons aiming to establish a revolutionary area and challenge the multinational companies devastating the tribal lands. Had I stayed to do my research I would have seen the transition and destruction of all the culture and tradition in the village where I had planned to stay.

But I was not destined to become an academic, although the journeys we made to remote mountain tribes were enthralling. We stayed in one village where I learned that although they might no longer practise human sacrifice, they did slaughter buffalo every year. This would have been unendurable for me, and in spite of my wild romanticism I could not see myself in reality spending lonely years isolated with people with whom I did not feel compatible. So with an apology to the spirit of Dame Eileen I returned to Bengal to spend more time with Bela.

Perhaps I should explain that over the last twenty years or so I have created my own fictive family, a companionship of fellow souls: Bela, Hilda, Nicola, Pat, Fran and Greta, among others, and in more recent years warriors in the animal rights movement such as my fictive brothers and mentors, Glenn, Ken, Les, Darren and Terry. Without this circle of free thinking colleagues and friends, all of whom share my passionate concern for animals, I would despair.

Bela belonged to a different, earlier era of my life. When she died in 1993, probably from the effects of chemical pesticides used on the village crops and draining into the water supply, it was a grievous loss to me. We had shared so much together during the Calcutta riots of 1946 when we were organising a midwifery service in the Bustees [slums] of Calcutta; and in our long journeys together to the villages to meet with Mahatma Gandhi during his fasts and prayer meetings. We used to sit on the pavement outside the Kali temple – dedicated to the goddess of smallpox – and vaccinate the devotees as they came out. Smallpox was endemic in Calcutta at that time.

I returned to Cambridge and resumed my career as a social worker, specialising as a Guardian ad Litem. Nicola started working in the National Health Service and has remained my dearest friend and my spiritual sister. I write this at her home in Bristol with her three cats, Hector, Pikka and Foss, as my helpers while Nicola keeps the NHS going as chief executive of a hospital in Bath. I trust her implicitly and long ago transferred my Cambridge house to her nominal possession as I was aware that being an animal rights activists could land one in deep financial trouble. Campaigners have had their homes and possessions seized by vengeful companies for security or to pay back the cost of damage inflicted during a protest. My solicitor was decidedly perturbed by this scheme, but I told him, 'She is not a family member, nor is it a lesbian relationship, but I know men cannot understand the bonds formed by women'.

Once I had put aside magical dreams of a career as an anthropologist, I found my new employment – as a Child Protection Officer, representing children as their Guardian ad Litem in court proceedings – quite enthralling.

We worked in partnership with a solicitor to represent children's welfare in contested cases in the family courts. In the early days we carried a degree of independence and autonomy which I suspect has now been bureaucratised and eroded. I commuted to London daily for the next ten years, interviewing children and their families, appointing specialists as necessary, to support the plan for the child's future – plans which did not inevitably agree with the views of the Social Services Department.

My work with children was often sad and distressing, but at least children have the protection of the law – unlike animals, where the law protects the interests of animal abusers and welfare codes are not worth the paper they are written on. Government bodies, vivisectors and others continually repeat the mantra that English law offers the greatest legal protection to animals in laboratories in the world, but we know from undercover investigations and from scientific documents that animals in laboratories are daily subjected to unbearable, degrading and sadistic torture in universities and research establishments. Many of the animals are driven mad, throwing into question the reliability of data produced as a result of such experiments. Again, factory farming laws and welfare codes are blatantly disregarded at markets, during transportation and live export and in the slaughterhouses. Everywhere that animals are enslaved they have no viable protection. It is not only incarcerated animals that are abused, but also wild creatures: foxes, deer, rabbits, hares, pheasant and fish all have their lives and habitat destroyed by hunting, trapping, shooting and fishing. William Blake wrote: "Everything that lives is holy," but our murderous species ignores the spiritual and moral value of animals.

In a way, my work in London helped to keep my life in balance as it is not possible to think only of animals when engaged in child protection. Fortunately my employers had not noticed that I was beyond the age of retirement, but when they did I had to retire – at the age of seventy-seven. My professional work, even before my retirement, went alongside my work for animal rights. My solicitor colleagues were amused and supportive, satisfied that so long as I produced reports on time and appeared in court as scheduled there was no conflict of interest.

Orissa tribal people at a wedding. The bride (in pink) is aged 13.

Chapter Three

Why?

All evolution in thought and conduct must first appear as heresy and misconduct.

George Bernard Shaw

I am always interested in what drives people to give their lives for animals. In my own life I have always liked to be at the frontier of change and to make an impact, questioning the established order when it is that of the oppressor. Kipling again, perhaps? Kim, who was the little friend of all the world. I also like to live a vivid life and am a born sensualist, preferring strong colours, strong perfumes and exciting action. Hence I prefer opera to all other music, provided it is tragic; Shakespeare's plays, ditto. John Curtin, an activist I have known for about twenty-five years and one of my moral advisors, once commented: "You are too addicted to flashing lights"; referring of course to the blue flashing lights of the numerous police cars that descend on every animal rights protest, regardless of public safety or disruption. I am one of those who 'enjoys a challenge', if I may use this cliché, and who takes a lead in social change as evidenced by my support for changes in the health services and in social work in this country and abroad as well as in political issues such as anti-war campaigns, protests against apartheid, the campaign for the abolition of hanging, and during the Second World War protesting hopelessly against oppression by putting up posters saying 'Save the Jews!'. There is great anger and outrage at the injustice and cruelty behind all this. My own childhood experiences were one motivating factor, but I dislike explaining all motivation in myself and others in psycho-dynamic terms, though my training biases me this way. But what gets built on the groundswell is another matter.

I was first influenced by the writing of Gandhi and Albert Schweitzer. Gandhi, in particular, was – and still is – the most compelling influence. I remember as a student nurse sixty-five years ago enlightening my colleagues in the ward kitchen as we raided the fridge. They told me to join the Quakers, which I did, drawn by their testimony of peace and their willingness to follow their conscience and pioneer social change. This led to many of them being imprisoned as conscientious objectors or refusing to take the oath in court. I drifted away from the Society of Friends for a variety of reasons and recently became a Buddhist, though keeping a spiritual investment in Christian teaching, drawn by the life and work of Jesus, the revolutionary message that inspired his followers to live dangerously, as he did, and to question power structures, and more than anything else his identification with the poor, like our street people in Cambridge, several of whom I regard as friends.

Most of my contacts in the animal rights movement shun any concept that what they do has any spiritual significance, probably because they confuse spirituality with the attitude of the Established Church, with its dark history of abusing animals, and the Roman Catholic Church's support for horrendous festivals where animals are tortured. For me, however, our work for the animals is a spiritual calling. The influence of Buddhism in my life started when I was in Calcutta in 1945, living in the Bustee area with my Hindu and Muslim friends, both during the riots and in more peaceful times. Buddhist monks came to visit me and invited me back to their Ashram to attend their ceremonies. I cannot now recall their specific orientation as there were many different communities. They invited me to join them, an attractive proposition both then and now, but I am too accustomed to comfortable living, though I willingly put up with serious discomfort when out campaigning.

In India I visited a number of Hindu and Buddhist sites with other team members of the Friends' Service Unit with whom I was working. We travelled by bus to see cave paintings in Ajanta, the amazing twenty-eight artificial cave temples carved out of the cliff face in the Indhyadri hills of East Maharastra. Each cave has an immense carving of the Buddha and beautiful murals carved out by reflected light in BC250. They were abandoned for centuries, then Mahanya monks (Bhiksu ordained members) renewed work on the carvings and occupied the caves for a time until in the seventh century they were abandoned again. They were accidentally rediscovered in 1889 by British army officers. We visited there long before the tourists and hippies arrived, and were the only visitors that day. The memory of those great statues still resounds in my mind, as does the curry we had for lunch that day at the Dak bungalow, consisting entirely of mild spiced green chillies! I did not know much about the teaching of the Buddha at that time, but what I did know continued to call me, particularly the concept of service to the afflicted and to all sentient beings.

Back in London following my time in India, I attended Buddhist meditation classes for a time. Then another visual impact came when I travelled overland to the Middle East and India in 1970. Staying in Kabul, we took a small plane to a place seventy-five miles northwest of the city, swooping over the mountains, (quite terrifying in a small plane) and landing at Bamiyan near the old silk route. I think being frightened is good for you, shakes up the system, increases your heart rate and is probably more advantageous than going to the gym. We clambered up the cliff to see the colossal figures of the Buddha. One was a hundred and seventy-seven feet tall, the largest stone statue in the world. Alas, having survived being defaced by Genghis Khan in AD122, they were ultimately destroyed by the fundamentalist Islamic Taliban regime in 2001. As I was lamenting about this to a Buddhist friend, he remarked "They were only stone". The destruction continues, with a massive trade in stolen artefacts dug up and exported all over the world, destroying a whole heritage of ancient religions and cultures. This happened again in the Baghdad museum only recently, including the destruction of the magnificent ancient harp, the originator of today's instrument.

In 2002 John Curtin organised a peaceful demonstration at Huntingdon Life Sciences, which he brilliantly called "*Meditate to Liberate!*"and invited people of all faiths. The Buddhists were represented by ordained members in their orange robes from the Amida Trust in Narborough. As a consequence of this contact I asked David Brazier, the spiritual director of the Amida Trust, to give a talk to a group I had organised for five years: "Animals, People and the Environment", an organisation designed to bring radical thinkers together, such as war resisters, women's rights, and the anti-Nestles' baby milk campaign, with the idea of acting as if there was still hope in the world. David Brazier, the Dharmavidya, is a man of intense intelligence and wisdom, a medical social worker, therapist and teacher with a PhD in Buddhism and an addiction to vegan ice cream discovered when he stayed with me for the first time.

I started reading more about Buddhist ethics and began to feel Buddhism was my natural spiritual home, so I telephoned David and asked him "How do I become a Buddhist?" He replied, "Say 'I'm a Buddhist'" and I did. He then said, "We have a little ceremony at our Bodhi centre in December which I'd be happy to talk to you about". And so in December 2004 I went up to the Amida Trust for the Retreat, which is the most important occasion and ceremony in the Buddhist year. I have been to one or two Anglican retreats where you sit quietly in your room in considerable comfort, sleeping and reading and being attended to by the nuns. I thought a Buddhist retreat would involve quiet moments of study in the library and perhaps elevating talks and periods of meditations, little knowing that a Buddhist retreat is a time of considerable asceticism, being called by a bell at 7 am, finishing about 9 pm with cocoa and biscuits, and pretty well non-stop apart from an hour's walk in the garden. I opted out of some of this, going to bed with a book, a resident cat and a hot water bottle, as is my custom. But after discussion with David I decided to take part in the ceremony known as 'Taking Refuge' and elected to take the Precepts, which included abstinence from alcohol and drugs. I hesitated about this, as well I might, since although I've never had any problems with addiction I liked to share an occasional powerful gin and tonic with friends. I also definitely liked vodka, to which I was introduced on a demonstration for the closure of the notorious Hillgrove cat breeding centre. Seeing me struggling up the hill, a friend offered me an iced vodka and orange from her flask and I never looked back. However, when I came home from the retreat, I gave away my cache of spirits and its absence has not bothered me since. Readers may know that some communities of Buddhists, especially Western Buddhists, do not take a vow of abstinence. Alas, now I shall never be able to have a cake made of magic mushrooms, having nervously put off trying them for so long and missing, I'm sure, an electrifying vision of the world.

I now belong to the Amida Trust. I am one of its patrons and have several friends in the community. Sustama sat with me in Oxford when I undertook a seventy-two hour fast in 2005. On the last day, the Dharmavidya appeared bringing me a blanket and a hot water bottle and stayed with me all day apart from the times when he vanished into bookshops.

Chapter Four

As long as the animals need me I'll be there.

Angela Walder

In 1978, as a second year student at New Hall, Cambridge, with preliminary exams behind me, I was less preoccupied with academic anxieties. The small terraced house I had purchased in the Petersfield area of Cambridge was conveniently close to the train station, the police station and the courts. This central position became very useful for animal rights campaigners, who were often released from cells in the middle of the night and in need of a bed. The house was also useful for media interviews. Robin Webb, press officer of the Animal Liberation Front, used it as an office extension, as did students struggling to write their PhDs.

That year I went to a protest in Trafalgar Square, a massive rally against the Canadian seal massacre which, alas, twenty-eight years later still continues. I was given a leaflet by Jean Pink, founder of Animal Aid, telling me of an Anti-Vivisection March that was going to be held in Cambridge. Jean Pink disappeared from the scene after a few years campaigning and is said to have joined an Ashram. This would not surprise me as people stop being animal rights activists for a variety of reasons: many become contemplative Buddhists and spend the rest of their lives meditating; some are seduced on to the property ladder with a house, a mortgage, marriage and the three piece suite; some become too depressed to carry on, or leave because of personality clashes; others devote themselves to welfare work, running much needed sanctuaries. It is not surprising that people drop out from activism or change their lives. The constant and increasing knowledge about animal suffering and each new atrocity we learn about is a blow to the heart. For example, millions of broiler hens are killed each year after a brief life of suffering. Yet we know that every hen has a personality of their own, and given a chance of freedom would soon show their individual character.

The first march in Cambridge, in 1978, was a landmark event. It was followed by a lecture by Hans Ruesch (author of *Slaughter of the Innocents*) who founded the Centre for Scientific Information on Vivisection in 1974. He illustrated the talk with slides showing some of the horrors of vivisection - rather too many, I thought, as excessive exposure tends to blunt one's feelings. Indeed, I think there is something vaguely sadistic about inflicting such terrible images on an audience of animal lovers. As a result of this event, the next day several of us met and founded Animal Aid Cambridge which was dedicated solely to opposing animal experiments. Even in those days we knew something of the torture inflicted on animals in the laboratories of the Departments of Anatomy, Physiology, Chemistry, Psychology, Bioscience etc on the Downing Street site. We quickly organised an all night vigil in Downing Street outside the entrance to the Department where animal experiments were carried out. The vigil was not particularly effective as there were only five of us and there was nobody about: we had not yet learnt the art of ensuring media publicity.

Our group expanded and at first it was organised in quite a conventional way, with regular speakers who extended our knowledge about animal abuse,

not only vivisection but hunting wild animals, live exports and the incarceration of live animals in zoos, safari parks and circuses. During the first few years we held these meetings at the local Friends Meeting House until they summarily evicted us because they knew we were involved in demonstrations at Huntingdon Life Sciences, where campaigners had pulled down the fences and invaded the premises. The occasion was described in the press as a "riot"

The Quakers are deeply invested in the peace movement, with their Peace Testimony and opposition to war. They have also pioneered many campaigns aimed at improving life for humans: prison reform, mental hospitals, and anti-slavery. One of their dicta is "Show a loving concern for all God's creatures", but there is little evidence of their concern for animals. Few are even vegetarians, and with several notable exceptions they are not involved in opposing even the worst institutional animal abuse such as factory farming or vivisection. They rationalise their non-involvement by condemning the actions of individuals in the radical animal liberation movement, as these involve destruction of property used to harm animals such as the trucks used to convey farm animals destined for the appalling live export trade. Quakers respect property, which is not surprising as most of them are comfortably off and middle class. So we moved to more welcoming premises at a Methodist church.

In those early days in the animal rights movement, as our knowledge increased we began to experiment with direct action as well as attempting to influence the public and make them more aware of what was happening. We had our first five-day fast in a church hall, drinking only herbal tea. Little I knew then of the possible poisoning effect of so much hibiscus! We hoped to make the churches more aware of our concerns, but I doubt whether we had much influence. The silence and palpable ignorance of many established churches in the face of so much animal suffering is quite enraging. Since that occasion we've had many fasts, drinking only water.

One of the early demonstrations we attended was at the Club Row market in London's East End. I once planned to write about the experiences of older women in the animal rights movement. One of the women I interviewed as part of this project was Angela Walder, a former lab technician and for the past twenty years an ARC campaigner. She provided the background in her account of the Club Row market:

"In 1978 I heard rumours about the street market at Club Row. Animal technicians from the laboratory where I used to work told me that animals from the market were sold to vivisection industries and that they cut the throats of kittens they couldn't sell and left them on the pavements. We held massive demonstrations every Sunday and on one occasion we pretended to be having a slanging match between ourselves as a diversion which gave other protesters a chance to rush over to the stalls and remove all the animals so that when the owners came back all the animals were gone, and quickly removed from the area leaving us to be arrested. We organized petitions and wrote endless letters to the Borough of Tower Hamlets, and padlocked ourselves to the railings outside the town hall. But Tower Hamlets wouldn't budge. We had support from Lord Houghton, a member of the House of Lords and a great campaigner for animals. He came up early one Sunday and was promptly arrested. I had promised his wife I would keep him safe and luckily the police released him quickly. Back in the House of Lords, he instigated a Bill to stop the sale of animals in street markets. Although we were often arrested we never served a prison sentence and in the cells we kept up our spirits by shouting out animal noises and in court we called ourselves White Rabbit, Black Rat, Beagle Dog etc, just to confuse them. The magistrates did not find this amusing.

Preaching at Worcester cathedral, Lord Houghton said, 'No social or political or moral change of any significance has been achieved in our country without it being thrust into politics, the pulpit and the police court. Christ was a dissenter and we follow him.'

Our first more challenging act in Cambridge, led by Angela Walder, was to chain ourselves to the railings of the Senate House in Cambridge in protest against vivisection. We refused to unlock ourselves, though actually my hands were shaking so my handcuffs were not properly locked anyway. We were bundled off in a police car in our first experience of arrest, with Hilda acting up as an old lady calling from her cell, "I want my tea and toast!"

Angela Walder
with rescued friends

Chapter Five

Hilda

"My heart sees her yet, my heart can't forget."

At about this time, in 1979, I met Hilda, another member of my fictive family. She was to become my constant companion until she died twenty years later in 1999. As is often the case with new friends, we met through a mutual love of cats. I went with her to feed the local feral cats, following her intrepid footsteps in the winter through snow and ice. Hilda was only five foot one inch tall, but her small body contained a valiant spirit. Going out with Hilda was very useful training for demonstrations and vigils, which often involved staying out all night in freezing weather. Hilda was a life affirming companion and although we had such different backgrounds her joie de vivre enlightened all our adventures and experiences together.

I also interviewed Hilda in about 1993, when she dictated her memoirs to me, including her account of her first demonstration at the Club Row market:

"I have lived in Cambridge all my life and in the same street for seventy years, until I moved to the next street to live opposite Joan. My father was a college porter and my mother a bed maker. I'm eighty-three years old now and had not been out of Cambridge, except for trips to Southend, until I met Joan. But now I've travelled all over the country on demonstrations, and around the world on holiday. I worked till I was sixty at Chivers jam factory, and as a cleaner. It was hard graft but I liked the work, it was nice company. I had a good family though we were very poor. I used to sweep up the horse manure in the street. I wanted to marry a gypsy but my sister and I decided not to get married when our father and brother died and we wanted to look after mother. Then my sister and my mother died so I was on my own until I got in with you lot.

I got to know about politics. We demonstrated outside Parliament and all over the place. I was a bit scared at first, especially when we chained ourselves outside the Senate House in 1982, but it was worth it because of the animals being vivisected in the University. I think experimenting on animals is dreadful, how can they be so cruel? Animals have feelings like us and we have no right to hurt them. We also demonstrated against the fur trade and got rid of it in Cambridge; they don't sell it here anymore. Sometimes we sat down in the department selling fur, or we went respectably dressed and put stink bombs under our shoes and on a given signal stepped on them, that soon cleared the shop, and I put chewing gum in the pockets of the fur coats. I like the Animal Liberation Front, because they get animals out of laboratories and do a lot of damage: serve the buggers right! Later we went to live export demonstrations and to lairages where they keep the poor sheep and lambs before loading them onto the transport trucks. I will never forget how they look at you and try to lick your hand: they trust you even though they are being betrayed. I also went with Joan into stinking battery hen units and saw them all crammed together. People who eat eggs deserve to get food poisoning.

They used to call me the cat lady round here. I feed all the strays and got them to the vet to be neutered. Well, I still feed them, but I'm no longer a little old lady in a head scarf, I'm more likely to wear a balaclava, riding about on my red tricycle that Joan got for me from an animal charity. I've always loved animals, I talk to all the dogs and cats I meet and pick up stranded snails and bees from the pavement and roads; why should they die? They have as much right to live as I have. But I didn't know much about animal abuse until I joined Animal Rights. The more you know the worse it gets. I wasn't even a vegetarian before and I think I got cancer from eating meat and stodgy food.

The first big national demonstration I went to was in 1983. I went with Joan to help Angela Walder, where she was campaigning to stop store holders selling pets at the Club Row market. They sold kittens and puppies and at the end of the day those they could not sell were chucked into bins. In the end we won."

My friendship with Hilda was founded on a passion for animals. At that time I had plenty of money working as a child protection officer in London, and together we went on the expensive adventures on safari and luxury holidays all round the world, to which I was addicted. Giving Hilda treats served as an excuse to indulge myself. That phase of my life is now finished due to old age, lack of cash and the knowledge of the environmental damage caused by tourism. And I cannot imagine travelling without Hilda.

Hilda

Hilda in Venice

Chapter Six

Direct Action

Power concedes nothing without a demand. It never did and it never will.
Tony Vernelli

During my professional career, I was always amused by my capacity to live a double life. One day I would be giving evidence in the High Court about child abuse and on another I would be challenging the law with regard to animal abuse with increasing confidence. My job taught me to stand up and present a case with confidence and to cope with cross-examination, often by the barrister representing social services, as the plan I proposed was often not in agreement with the social services.

Social workers at that time were often reluctant to place a child in need of care with his grandparents, reasoning that if the grandparents' daughter or son abused their child, then there must have been something wrong in the family upbringing. But this is not necessarily the case, particularly in Caribbean families where it is customary for grandparents to take care of grandchildren. On occasion, I supported the wishes of lesbian or gay couples to foster or adopt a child, or opposed a plan to remove a child from their care. One little boy told me, "it's quite okay to have two mothers, and I'm not gay. Would you like to meet my girlfriend?"

When I was young I was totally phobic about speaking in public. But because my work entailed addressing courts and teaching commitments, the fear was more than overcome. So now I relish public life and being in the limelight in defence of animals. The only problem is that I hate having to dress up and wear a bra for television interviews. I continued to combine my professional life with caring for animals, and on one occasion, I carried a flea-ridden tortoiseshell cat in a box into the High Court, rescued from a dilapidated high-rise flat. One of the ushers kindly looked after her until I was free. You couldn't do that nowadays for fear the cat was hiding a bomb. Sixteen years later, Molly is still living happily ever after with a friend of mine on this very street.

Thinking about our ability to deal with the media, the Animals Rights movement can be a great education in many ways. Pat, my valued colleague, was too shy to read out the minutes in a meeting in 1980, but now she's one of the most eloquent of our group. Pat and Sue and I call ourselves the "gran-archists". Before I was made to retire at the age of 77, I could not risk being arrested. But Hilda had no such qualms. Her first raid with the Animal Liberation Front (ALF) was to take part in a release of mice and rats from a local research institution.

"It was just as you can imagine, a barely lit long shed, with tiers and rows and rows of cages. You would have thought I would have difficulty choosing which to take, but I didn't hesitate and grabbed several. Alas, I dropped one in the field and the mice escaped, but I didn't stop and thought at least they would have their moment of freedom. We packed the cages into the back of the van and I sat with them, covered in cages. My cats were disgusted when I got home, especially Tiddles, who said I 'smelt' revolting.'

Later that week outside the Cambridge Union, which I was attending for a debate, I asked the policemen standing outside the door if they were waiting for protesters. "No", they said, "We're looking for 600 escaped mice."

Hilda went on to join a group that raided Laundry Farm in Cambridge, which supplied dogs for transplant operations. These were not purpose-bred dogs as they would be now and there is every reason to assume they were strays. Hilda told me later that it was pouring with rain, and I'm surprised she did not sink into the mud as she clambered over the fields. "They had to carry me for the last lap," she said. I saw her when I got back from work: her boots and jeans were soaked in mud. "Throw them out, for goodness' sake,' I commanded, 'They're incriminating.' But the rescuers were never caught and Hilda fell in love with her rescued dog, a Rhodesian Ridgeback, who sat in the back of the car as they fled to London and his new home, his long muzzle resting trustingly on her shoulder. Hilda said, "You know, they never barked when they came out, they just jumped up and down with joy and licked our faces as we fixed the lead on them, as if they knew the danger of getting caught."

Raids on laboratories were common in the 1980s, but laboratories and research centres in this country are now heavily guarded, though massive rescues take place in Europe, the USA and even in Russia.

We continued to be involved with direct action and went regularly to Liverpool Street to protest at a particularly gruesome chicken slaughterhouse, which I believe is now closed. Local people would queue up for a chicken which was killed on the spot, shoved into a plastic bag and handed to the buyer for their Sunday lunch. One day, when I had to stay at home, a friend rang me from Liverpool Street saying he was bringing several guests for tea. I didn't twig what he meant at first and just told him "Fine". After he rang off I remembered what he was doing that day. Tony arrived at four o'clock with seven boxes, each containing a hen. Hilda said, "You can put them in my front room". We opened the boxes, gave the thirsty birds some water and corn and let them loose. "Put some newspaper down if you don't mind," said Hilda, "I just got that carpet on the insurance."

Our next call was to a friend – there is always a friend on these occasions – and she came to collect them the next day. She put them in her shower room, where they promptly destroyed the curtain, before going to their new homes over the next couple of days. It is astonishing how quickly rescued hens recover from their ordeals, even when you take them from battery farms: within a few hours they are pecking away at the ground. It is simply not true that you cannot rehabilitate most animals. When we first packed up the birds we only found six and thought we must have miscounted. A week later, tidying up the room, Hilda found a hen hiding behind the radiator. "She looks okay," she said, "but it just goes to show, you should count your chickens."

Deeply disturbed by the disgusting conditions in factory farms, we decided to visit a battery farm. Nothing had prepared us for the noise, heat and smell. The workers were busy snatching birds two at a time by their feet and throwing them into cages in transport trucks which would take them to their final end. One hen had fallen on the floor during the ruthless dispatch of these end-of-lay birds. We picked her up and brought her swiftly home. She was heat-exhausted and I was doubtful whether she would live. But Glenn, a brilliant physicist and my number one fictive brother, whom I call the archangel Gabriel because of his ravishing good looks, fanned Henrietta, as we called her, and wiped her with a damp cloth. 'I'm afraid she's not going to make it' he said. But she did. Once she was cool and hydrated we took her to Elizabeth Anderson's farm where she lived for years, roosting on the back of an old sheep called Barley. "She smells so nice of lanoline", said Elizabeth. Henrietta lived to a great old age. So too did Barley, until at the end Elizabeth had to lift the sheep on to his arthritic feet. The day came when he had to be put to sleep. "I buried him with Henrietta in the centre of my other animal graves and put a sundial over them".

Henrietta and Barley

Elizabeth Anderson and Henrietta

We have mounted rather ineffective demonstrations outside intensive chicken and turkey farms and on Christmas Day we like to join our Kings Lynn friends with a vegan lunch in the grounds of Bernard Matthews. On occasion, we followed this up by visiting the turkey farms, but this is no longer possible as these travesties of farms are so heavily guarded that direct action may not be possible or contribute as much to their downfall as exposure by undercover filming. These exposés, subsequently shown in documentaries on TV, have helped to pressurise supermarkets, who want to keep up a good public image in their phoney desire to depict themselves as carers of food welfare. For example, notice was taken of our campaign about hock burns to broiler chickens, caused by the birds being unable to stand due to bone disease: their bones cannot stand their heavy weight, so they struggle along on their wings in ammonia-soaked litter.

There are those who disagree with any attempt to reduce suffering of animals in captivity as they think this may encourage the trade to continue, for example in promoting free range eggs and forgetting all the male chicks who are suffocated at birth. I remain unclear about my own position on this issue, other than in promoting veganism. The public are misled. Free range chickens are very rarely actually free range and will still be slaughtered. But until the great day of Animal Liberation, I do welcome any chance to relieve the present suffering of animals so I give some rather half-hearted support to national organisations, such as Compassion in World Farming and the RSPCA who pursue this path, though clearly they accept that as people eat meat, the animals' welfare must be improved. But I would rather give my time and energy to organisations such as Viva! who condemn the whole bloody business of eating animals or their products.

As the months and years went by we began to learn much more about animal abuse, not only about vivisection. In many other areas of the country we campaigned to stop local authorities from allowing circuses with wild animals on council land. We succeeded, as did many other campaigners, but we have not been able to stop them appearing on public land. We used such tactics as we could, taking down notices, booking seats that we did not intend to take up, and Hilda and others went around the city pasting 'cancelled' over the posters. None of us felt brave enough really to protest in the circus, but one young boy volunteered to do so. When the elephants came on, he shouted out and pretended to vomit. Sadly neither he nor his mother were well treated by the audience, who pushed them out quite roughly. You have to be careful at circuses as the owners can be quite rough too. There have been some improvements. In 1999 there were twenty-five circuses using animals as entertainment, now there are only nine. The Animal Rights movement has campaigned successfully to get them barred from council land. One of the remaining nine, the "Great British Circus", still has five performing tigers, claiming this helps to preserve the species!

We also got heavily involved with the campaign against fur farms, which were banned by the British government in January 2003. All over the country activists were liberating mink, as indeed they are now in Europe. We went up to Cock Sparrow Farm near Coventry, which bred beautiful arctic foxes for the fur trade. A coachload of us invaded the property, and on the first visit the police were surprisingly non-interventionist. The campaigners smashed the holding sheds and machinery, broke open the deep-freezers and generally caused mayhem. I took the office keys and gave them to someone I thought could make use of them. Hilda, all five foot of her, was lifted up by a helpful policeman, so she could have a good look at the foxes. One of the group removed a fox and carried it off, not surprisingly being bitten on the way to her car. On the way back to the coach, Hilda picked up a cabbage or two from the breeder's field, "It'll do for your rabbits Joan," she said, never one to miss an opportunity. I, of course, discouraged such rampant vandalism.

Fur farms are now banned, but Britain is the biggest trader of fur in the world, and plays an important role in the European seal fur trade. The British Fur Trade Association states that the UK trade in animal furs is worth between £400 million and £500 million per year.

In England the most popular furs are mink, fox and rabbit. Shops do not sell seal fur but seal products worth about £300,000 per year get imported into this country and then exported around the world. Seal penises are on sale as traditional Chinese medicine, prized as an aphrodisiac.

Sadly, fur from cats and dogs is also imported. Although this is deplored by the government, it is not yet banned. As a small campaigning group, we cannot respond to every instance of animal abuse but we do react to local issues, support national campaigns, write letters to the Press and to Government agencies and sign petitions, and we are active campaigners on national campaigns.

Chapter Seven

Live Exports

"From the cradle to the grave, the lives of farm animals are a living hell"

Keith Mann: *From Dusk 'til Dawn*

I officially retired at the age of 77 when I ceased work as a guardian ad litem. Retirement is a dangerous time. Psychologically, work structures one's life – particularly if it is as interesting as mine has been. In the final five years or so, I was beginning to find it physically fatiguing. I was working in London, and at the end of the day I would emerge from the Underground at Kings Cross with a profound sense of relief, grasping an iced vodka and a houmous sandwich and heading for the Cambridge train on the platform now famous for the Harry Potter Hogwarts Express, which leaves from Platform 9 3/4. I usually found a seat, but if the train was crowded I would wait for the next one. Once on board, I joined other exhausted commuters and fell asleep straight away.

Sometimes I had a box on my lap containing a few guinea pigs or rats, released from their life of hell in some unnamed laboratory or breeding centre en route for new homes, which I had collected from an animal rights activist at the station. On one occasion I stowed my briefcase up on the rack and was suddenly nudged by a City gentleman sitting beside me who had been showered with pigeon feed from the broken bag on to his spotless shirt. I apologised profusely. "You don't look the type" he said, glancing at my box of animals and my smart work attire. "No, I'm probably more suited to the Hogwarts Express," I replied. He looked puzzled for a moment, then brushing the seed from his jacket said, "Ah, a Harry Potter fan – those books keep my family together", "Saves going to Relate," I commented, and fell asleep again.

Without work, and thinking that a life entirely centred on animal rights could be psychologically damaging, I enrolled for another degree and started classes in feminism at the University of East Anglia. After two sessions I decided it was not for me. I do not like modules, or the pressure of over-organised education, particularly after studying at the University of Cambridge, where you are left to get on with it, sink or swim, provided you get your essays in on time and attend your supervision sessions.

The time I spent on animal rights activities increased very rapidly, as did my family of cats and rabbits. I specialise in elderly or disabled cats, currently seven of them, who live comfortably in my home on electrically heated bedding or in my double bed. My beloved Siamese, Wilhelmina, sleeps on my shoulder at night and we breathe the same air. "So unhealthy," someone once remarked, to which I responded, "But she doesn't seem to catch any germs from me". Pushkin and Suki, who moved with me to Cambridge from London both lived until they were 17 and are still much missed.

The two rescued New Zealand rabbits, liberated from a life of hell, have a one hundred foot garden paradise and enjoy pulling down the roses, hiding in the long grass, digging burrows under the cherry tree, and chasing the cats away if they intrude on their space. They do this by circling around the cat until it gets disoriented and dashes back through the cat flap. Poppy, who lost her tail in a dreadful accident before she came to live with me, thinks she is a rabbit and nuzzles up to them. Despite being constantly rejected by them, she still prefers to sleep in their hutch.

In the mid 1990s, the main campaign was against live exports. Dover temporarily banned the trade because of public outcry, so the exporters moved to the ports of Brightlingsea, Shoreham and Kings Lynn. They also flew calves out by air through Coventry. It was at Brightlingsea that so many previously law-abiding "respectables" joined the movement, confusing the media, who prefer to describe us as a "rent-a-mob", "out of work scroungers", "anarchists" and, more recently, "terrorists". The sight of endless truckloads of bewildered animals going through the narrow streets inspired the Brightlingsea Against Live Exports campaign. It was a sickening experience as we could see the victims on the trucks, look into their eyes, and smell their fear and panic. There are few words to describe this cruelty. But at least human beings can find the language, whereas animals have no coherent words, though they try to communicate with us. We know that many are driven mad in research laboratories, and this causes brain damage. The animals sent for slaughter probably also have toxins in their bodies which may well damage those people who still eat their flesh.

At the ports, protesters ran in front of the trucks and were dragged away by the police, who seemed particularly fond of manhandling young girls, pulling them away by their hair and earrings.

When the live export trade moved back to Dover, where it continues still, protesters from all over the country rallied round, led by committed protesters. A local group and Carla Lane monitored the trade, regardless of weather conditions. In the *Sunday Telegraph* in 1999 Carla described how, when her sanctuary was more adequately staffed, she could be more active in Dover.

"I now have time to attend to my real passion, the campaign against the live export trade. One day when I ran alongside the animal trucks on their way to the port, with a banner in one hand, a loud-hailer in the other, a whistle between my teeth and icicles in my hair, a policeman picked me up and tossed me over the hedge. From the prison cell I wrote to my sons to explain that when I died their only inheritance would be the house, because the rest of my money would be swallowed up in running the sanctuary and campaigns."

We found the demonstrations at Dover heart-rending. We stood helplessly as truck after truck rolled down the hills filled with tier upon tier of sheep or pigs, stinking of ammonia. We knew the cruel fate that awaited them in Europe or beyond, a holocaust in the terrible slaughterhouses. At the lairages, we watched sheep being loaded up, and tried not to meet the sad eyes of the matriarch sheep standing at the head of her flock. Sheep remember their friends and family. In his book, *Pleasurable Kingdom*, Jonathan Balecombe, an animal behaviour research scientist with the Physicians Committee For Responsible Medicine, quotes evidence that sheep can recognise fifty or more members of their flock from photographs of their faces and keep this memory for two years. He bases this on the extensive research of Kenrick et al, published in November 2001, and by *Animal Welfare* magazine in the same year. He gives many other examples of the cognitive and emotional intelligence of animals, so people who talk about their companion animals saying "They understand every word I say" are probably not far wrong. Not only are sheep exposed to unbearable suffering, but they also grieve for their friends and companions. I like to think that I still believe in non-violent protests, but in my heart I rejoice when I read that an animal transport truck has been burnt by the ALF.

In the mid-1990s I organised a five-day hunger strike outside the Ministry of Agriculture, with placards and leaflets to distribute to passers by. I have a cynical view of men who have ties and never take leaflets, but in fact many MPs were supportive, including of course Tony Banks, an animal rights activist who, alas, died not long ago. During our fast, he either visited us every day or sent his secretary to make sure we were all right. Carla Lane drove by in her car, blasting a message on her megaphone. This fast was singularly uncomfortable, with fumes from buses (we were just by a bus stop), uncertain weather – blazing hot sunny days and cold nights – and our inadequate protection against the weather, as most of us are unnatural campers. All this, combined with hunger, made the protest quite an ordeal. But it also attracted a lot of publicity and we ended in good spirits, enjoying food brought by Nitin Mehta, the Jain leader of the Young Indian Vegetarians.

Following our fast, Compassion in World Farming organised a daily protest at the Ministry. Although I believe we should do all we can to influence Parliament, and use what is left of our rapidly diminishing democratic rights to campaign legally, in my heart I believe it is direct action that carries the day. This has certainly been the case in all other social revolutions.

"My life changed", 52 year old Daphne told me in Dover. "I couldn't believe what was happening. I met with Jessica, aged 76, and we campaigned together. It was a scene from hell at the docks. I was so outraged that I became a full-time activist. Animals are made by God. I believe they have souls, even the ants, and when they die they go to Paradise. I think about animals all the time."

Most animal rights campaigners say they are not religious, but I am convinced that they have a sense of a profound spiritual calling. As Lisa says, "They must be all around us in the animals' parallel universe. I am driven to fight for the animals. It gives you power. It's a life force." One thing is certain: we are all united in our empathy with animals and with the blazing anger against their tormentors and against the injustices inflicted on them.

The situation often seems hopeless, as when the transport of baby calves to Europe in veal crates was resumed in 2006. We are encouraged by small victories, such as the banning of paté de foie gras in Israel; in

Austria vulnerable animals have a legal advocate; and in Rome goldfish bowls have been banned and dog owners are compelled to exercise their dogs. The production of foie gras in the UK is banned, but not its import, so we continue to campaign against shops and restaurants in the UK that still sell it. The recent Animal Welfare Act may help some distressed animals by giving more power to the RSPCA, but it offers no protection to invertebrates such as lobsters and octopuses. It is also dispiriting to realise that veterinary surgeons are often the servants of animal torturers. Vets are supposed to monitor the disgusting trade in live exports, animals in factory farms, and in slaughterhouses and markets, and they would no doubt argue that these are legal activities. If more vets had a conscience, they would speak up against institutionalised animal cruelty, instead of which they rubber-stamp the forms, take a cursory look at some of the animals, and pocket the cheque.

The same could be said of doctors who have been implicated in the torture of human beings during the unspeakable events of the Holocaust, which have many parallels with the institutionalised cruelty to non-human animals. As for medical research on human beings, there were experiments on patients dying of liver disease in 1950, and many other examples in America. As Helen Bamber wrote in her article "A Life against Cruelty" in *The Good Listener*: "Many physicians have become scientists rather than healers, and inflict pain on confused and weakened people to confirm some banal result."

Once people and animals are regarded as commodities, they are at the mercy of those who exploit them. Over the years we would never have known what goes on in factories or laboratories, circuses and slaughterhouses, if it was not for the ALF and undercover agents such as Sarah Kite who worked as an investigator for eight months in Huntingdon Life Sciences in 1989, penetrating their high security and exposing the secret world of suffering there. It was following her exposé that the animal rights campaign became much more radical and active in its efforts to close the centre down. There have been many other undercover investigators in this country, the rest of Europe and the USA, not only in vivisection institutes but also in the factory farms, exposing the suffering of poultry, pigs, ducks, and the filthy conditions in which they live in chronic pain from fractures and disease.

Other campaigners have concentrated on what is described as 'market watch', spending months watching and recording what happens to animals sold in markets. I joined fellow campaigners at the Bury St Edmunds market protest where the animals were left without water. We held all-night vigils there and also attended meetings of the local council, standing with our banners behind the councillors and interrupting proceedings by shouting, "Water for the animals!" We poured a jug of water over the chairman's head. "That's not necessary,' he remarked. But later, to his credit, he came out and talked to us. The market was sickening. I hated the notice which said "spent cattle", packed with poor exhausted cows who had spent their lives producing milk, not for their own babies but for human beings.

At last it seems that nutritionists and doctors are looking at evidence which may indicate a link between drinking cow's milk and illnesses such as prostate cancer, eczema, diabetes and other diseases, particularly allergies. When I went for a breast cancer check, the consultant said "You're a vegan – we've never had a case of breast cancer in a vegan." Cow's milk contains growth hormones that are particularly dangerous to humans.

If people are oblivious to the physical and mental suffering of cows – of whom a quarter have mastitis and are in chronic pain, living a life of perpetual childbirth and lactation, mourning their babies who are taken away almost at birth – they may finally give up drinking milk when they become more aware of the risks to their own health.

Chapter Eight

Vivisection

'Terrors are turned upon me, they pursue my soul as the wind; and my welfare passes away as a cloud.'

Job, 30:15

In the mid 1990s, the focus of the animal rights movement moved from live exports to the anti-vivisection campaign, and this may well continue until animal experimentation ceases. We need a real sea-change in the scientific community with its blinkered ignorance of the value of non-animal testing. Until that happens, we shall pursue the victories already achieved from campaigns and from the steady but spectacular progress made by Europeans for Medical Progress and more recently by Oxford academics and spiritual leaders, who have proved over and over again that using animals as models for research places humans at risk.

The side effects of prescribed drugs frequently cause more pain and distress than the disease itself. [2]A concerned NHS executive has estimated that drug side-effects could be causing "70,000 deaths and cases of severe disability in England each year - putting Adverse Drug Reactions behind only heart disease and stroke as a cause of death". I understand that on post-mortem reports the cause of death is stated as the main disease, such as cancer or heart failure, but in fact the patient may have died from the side effects of treatment. The lethal side effects of prescribed drugs such as Vioxx, Amrinone, or Alzheimer's vaccine and many others have been graphically described in the *British Medical Journal* (15/12/06)

---

2   Uncaged.co.uk.

In the mid-1990s, animal rights campaigners concentrated their energy on Hillgrove, a farm near Oxford which bred a thousand cats for vivisection. We had already seen the end of Shamrock, a primate breeding centre near Brighton, where we held vigils throughout the freezing winter in driving rain and snow. We could smell the poor incarcerated creatures. When we returned from these demonstrations, often soaked to the skin and freezing cold, we felt guilty soaking in hot baths, making tea and turning up the heating, knowing that hour by hour, day by day, sometimes for years, enslaved non-human animals remain at the mercy of their tormenters. Many campaigners have been arrested on these demonstrations, and continue increasingly to spend their time in police stations and prison, but they are always supported by their friends and the Vegan Prisoners Support Group, which ensures that vegan prisoners are properly fed, and that their families and companion animals are properly cared for.

The Hillgrove campaign inspired rage, anger and energy. It was particularly poignant, of course, as so many of us love cats and value their companionship. The Hillgrove cats were supplied to laboratories in this country and also exported to Japan. Week after week we descended on Hillgrove, a farmhouse surrounded by woods and turnip fields. The campaign was led by Natasha, Heather and Greg, whose lives are totally dedicated to animal rights despite having served and continuing to serve long prison sentences. Many of these demonstrations led to riotous activities with enraged campaigners tearing down the fences, throwing mud and stones at the building, pursued by riot police on foot and horseback. On more than one occasion I was dragged into a ditch by one little girl I was supposed to be looking after. Eventually the farmer gave up under our continued attacks, which included intimidation of his workers and suppliers. Before this happened a number of cats were liberated by the ALF, who climbed through the roof. Tragically some were arrested with rescued cats. The cats were returned to Hillgrove by the police, where they would have been destroyed because they were no longer in a sterile condition. I cannot imagine how rescuers survived and kept their sanity in such circumstances. I know one who did not and is still struggling through the dark winters of depression.

To my joy, one rescued cat came to me. A girl telephoned saying, "Look outside your door in an hour - I'm leaving you a present." And so I acquired the utterly beautiful grey cat, Emily. She was little more than a kitten and terrified, disappearing under the bed. Fortunately she was too young to have been tattooed, so I did not have to arrange for it to be removed. After a while she settled happily, loved by my other cats, spending happy hours on the kitchen table, curled up on a circular tray covered by a pad overlapping the radiator, and turned into a truly beautiful cat. She told me that her grandmother was a Russian blue, which accounted for her double thick coat. After about a year, when trust was established, she would roll over on her back, showing me her lovely white belly, curling up her paws. So the game of 'curly paws' enchanted my friends and her adoring public. My Siamese, Wilhelmina, made friends with her, recognizing another pedigree. Like me, she is an elitist. Had Emily stayed at Hillgrove, she would probably have been sent as a breeding queen to Japan, if not to a British vivisector, one of whom remarked at a conference, "I prefer to use cats for my experiments - they are cheaper than primates." Emily was quite young, but like so many rescued cats, her teeth began to cause her pain, so she went to our trusted local vet to have them removed. On that day Ken, Alice and I were sitting drinking chocolate in the cybercafé when the vet telephoned. Ken, looking very white, told me that Emily had died under the anaesthetic. "We'll go and fetch her and bring her back home." The vet was extremely distressed too, but I learned later that many Hillgrove cats

Emily

had heart problems from inbreeding and that others had also died. Beautiful Emily, you purred your way into our hearts and I trust your curly paws will meet me when I come to greet you.

When Hillgrove closed, and the farmer returned to his turnip field, the RSPCA removed all the cats, and found no difficulty in finding them homes, taking all the credit for this. I personally never thought we'd see the end of this establishment, so our victory was a great joy.

Chapter Nine

Huntingdon Life Sciences

As effective as mass demos can be, the protest is still a public demonstration of public disapproval and outrage. I believe our movement needs to do more than just protest, we need to unapologetically work towards the financial ruin of Huntingdon Life Sciences and every other single business that profits from death and destruction from the natural world... Huntingdon Life Sciences a vivisection laboratory that today represents all the evil that has sought to reduce animals to genetically mapped and manipulated machines and reduce the homeland they came from to a wasteland.

Rod Coronado, Archangel, Issue 28: Warrior Nation

Sarah Kite worked undercover at Huntingdon Life Sciences (HLS) – at that time called Huntingdon Research Centre – for eight months, penetrating their high security, and her subsequent exposé of the terrible suffering of the animals there was given coverage by the BBC in their programme 'It's a Dog's Life'. This gruesome establishment specialises in toxicology – i.e. the poisoning of animals – which first became known to the public through their tobacco experiments on beagles. They claim to advance medical research, but in fact their main work is not on medical research but testing sun lotion, artificial sweeteners, paints, dyes and food additives, and to get these toxic products on the market HLS kills thousands of animals, including primates, horses, mice, rats, dogs, cats, fish, birds, monkeys, guinea-pigs, rabbits and ferrets.

Our local group organised marches, hunger strikes and vigils, and theatrical mock funerals carrying coffins labelled: "Animals killed at Huntingdon Research Centre". We sat in front of the coaches carrying workers until the angry drivers shouted, "We have to get these people to work, and we're not stopping for you!" and usually we were hauled away by the police. In any case we decided it was too dangerous, remembering the tragic death of Jill Phipps who was killed in 1995 under the wheels of a truckload of calves destined for live export in Coventry.

In 1988, Huntingdon Research Centre was not defended as it is now, resembling a high security prison with six-foot railings topped with razor wire, high security cameras, watchtowers and floodlights. Our campaigns in the 1980s were very moderate compared with those of more recent history, but police restrictions now make it almost impossible to have effective demonstrations at the site, which resembles a Nazi concentration camp. There are other similarities: Huntingdon Life Sciences is a concentration camp for non-humans, destroying 500 animals every day.

In 1998, a new group called "Stop Huntingdon Animal Cruelty" (SHAC) emerged, led by Natasha, Heather and Greg Avery who had successfully led the campaign against the Hillgrove cat breeding 'farm' and who now spearheaded the campaign against HLS using focused and highly successful tactics.

We welcomed them, as in the preceding years we had made very little impact on this gruesome establishment. In *The Guardian* (1st June 06) Greg Avery, aged 38, told how the group had waged a seven-year campaign to close down HLS. They have been very successful in their war against this big business through their extensive knowledge of how the City works. Their research helped them to focus on hitting the company financially and they got information on all the shareholders and the names of the big investment bankers who supported HLS – including the Labour Party Pension Fund, who quickly sold their shares after demonstrations outside the homes of their directors. SHAC learned that HLS banked with NatWest (later taken over by the Royal Bank of Scotland) and had huge loans from these banks. They also targeted Market Makers, who pulled out, and HLS shares on the London Stock Exchange were suspended.

SHAC focused on persuading suppliers of the laboratory to withdraw their custom. They used intimidation as a weapon at times, although they usually tried to explain to the supplier what was actually going on at Huntingdon Life Sciences. Eventually even the crematorium that cremated the pathetic victims eventually refused to deal with Huntingdon Life Sciences when they realised it did not go down well with customers who used the pet cemetery and the pet crematorium.

We obtained shares in HLS and so were able to attend AGMs in London and disrupt them. When they moved the AGM to Boston in the USA I was still able to go with one of my 'brothers', Terry. With all the new government and police restrictions, it is unlikely that we would be able to do this so effectively now. We supported the demonstrations at the banks, especially NatWest in Cambridge and in the City of London. We would walk into the banks and sit on the counters until asked to leave by the police. I was only in my seventies at that time and thus much more agile than I am now, but even then I found it quite alarming to be followed by plain clothed policemen down the streets and into the tube stations, up and down escalators, jumping from one train to the other in the hope of eluding them, explaining to fellow passengers what it was all about. I begun to feel like a fugitive in an American film and slightly alarmed. I even considered getting off at Liverpool Street and straight on to the next train back to Cambridge, but eventually I escaped my pursuers and rejoined the protest.

Events in the campaign moved so fast that I find it quite difficult to keep to any chronological format. In 1999, we established our first protest camp outside the laboratories. The camps were organised by experienced radicals, some of whom came from other ecological campaigns, and were led by John Curtin.

The whole experience was amazing for a novice like me. I had long admired this form of direct, non-violent protest undertaken by Earth First road protesters, tree-huggers, anti-war camps and the amazing demonstrations by the women's camps at Greenham Common. We established our legal right to squat on the land and Terry Woods (my fifth 'brother') dug out a deep cave, later to be occupied for three days by Greta, who was blocked in by a heavy safe, her only companion a spider, until the police released her and she was escorted to Holloway. Actually the safe was not locked, but the police believed it was and spent three days trying to dig her out. When this proved too difficult, they called in a specialised caving team. A young Finnish girl took up residence in a tree house, and we established a cooking area, tents, and a superior earth loo. John's beautiful greyhound, Brian, ran around happily while activists arrived with wood for the fire, barricades and food. On at least one occasion the rooftops of the research centre were scaled. We kept up a continual demonstration to inform local people and the media why we were there.

In our first protest camp – there were three in all – it was quite nerve racking, never knowing when the bailiffs would arrive. We took turns on watch but were not always as alert as we should be. One night those on guard were asleep, but luckily Pat and Sue were awake and roused us. There were row upon row of men clad in yellow waterproofs and police in black riot gear at the gates. There was a frantic rush for people to take up their defence positions and the arm holds, and Greta dived into her cave. I disentangled myself from Brian the greyhound's embrace and groped under the camp bed, blindly searching for my glasses and a missing shoe, assisted by Sue who is often at hand when I'm disoriented.

But then, looking as ever impressive and cool, I stayed guard to poke up the fire and put on the kettle, and told the sheriff's men we would not move until we'd had tea. Protesters in armlocks and Greta were dragged away by the police, and we were told to get moving, but we didn't hurry, taking our time, packing up the camp into trucks. I noticed how my friends carefully moved beetles and other insects whom we had disturbed to a safe place in the woods. This tender regard is typical of animal rights activists and never ceases to touch my heart. I remember Ken, for instance, bringing an injured frog to my pond. Watching from the window I saw him crouched down by the water, giving gentle artificial respiration to his patient. "I don't think he's going to make it,' he said, gently rubbing its throat. What with the beetles and the loading up it was some time before we drove away from Camp Remus, as we called it, and we were sad to go. Huntingdon Life Sciences quickly moved in, chopped down our tree, bought up all the land to prevent us camping again and enclosed the area with barbed wire. But we had achieved massive publicity, and cost the vivisectors immense sums estimated to be in excess of a million pounds, including the cost of the land and additional security. We established two more camps until we were finally driven away.

Tea Party!

49

Camp

Hilda and a friend had an amusing time one Christmas when they heard that it was quite simple to get in on the Huntingdon Life Sciences works coach. She and her friend got on the bus at Huntingdon carrying Christmas shopping and sat down quietly. They were surprised not to be challenged and bemused to find themselves carried through the gates with other workers. They donned white coats and spent the day rather aimlessly, not being experienced ALF campaigners, but taking notes of what they saw. As Hilda said, "It was impossible to get to the animals. We could hear the dogs barking, and smell them." But she had one surprising success, placing a neat package in the director's tray, with a label wishing him a Happy Christmas. After we left they called in the Bomb Squad and blew it up. They were not amused when the box exploded dog biscuits over the entire office. There was a police investigation afterwards, but no one was charged.

We did not know at the time that baboons and other primates were being used for terrible experiments in xeno-transplantation research programmes carried out by a firm called Imutran, transplanting organs or tissue from one species of animal to another. In May 2000, brave activists removed all the research documents and study reports from the Imutran offices in Trumpington and photocopied them. The documents were sent to an anti-vivisection group called Uncaged who for the next two years worked on exposing the appalling suffering of the primates, calling their campaign reports *Diaries of Despair*. The following is an extract from an account by Dr Dan Lyons, Director of Uncaged:

"The documents revealed in graphic detail the horrific fate of some five hundred higher primates – the cousins of human beings – as they were transported thousands of miles to face certain death in the experiments, conducted at the notorious Huntingdon Life Sciences' establishment. For the first time, we at Uncaged believed we could present the raw facts about animal experiments. There would be no room for spin or obfuscation – the researchers themselves told in their own words how monkeys and baboons died in fits of vomiting and diarrhoea, spasms and body tremors, seeping wounds and bloody discharges, grinding teeth and uncontrollable eye movements... or just quiet and huddled as they sickened and were 'sacrificed', to use the cold parlance of the animal labs"

The full report is included at Appendix 1, and the supporting documents, *Diaries of Despair* report and analysis can be seen at www.xenodiaries.org.

I knew a lot about this exposé and sent copies of the evidence to our local MP and others who totally ignored it. But Dr Dan Lyons and his partner Angela never gave up and now the information is in the public domain, which all goes to show what two people with tenacity, courage and integrity can achieve. It is similar to the campaign fought by the McLibel duo against the huge McDonalds corporation, causing much grief and financial loss.

Once our group knew what happened to the primates at HLS we organised local demonstrations to alert the public to the cruelty and the dangers of xeno-transplantation. We staged marches and 'die-ins' where people would lie down in the grounds of Imutran and be put in plastic sacks like victims dying from retro-virus infections. It was so effective that in the doom-laden atmosphere two people passed out and one policeman went so pale he almost fainted till I gave him a glass of water to revive him. I've heard with alarm that similar experiments are likely to continue, using genetically modified pigs – poor things!

As a result of the campaign, much of the Imutran's business has been transferred to America, where they are now being effectively targeted by American campaigners. Their terrible experiments on baboons have not led to any improvement in human health.

SHAC have been so effective that HLS have had to sell their research laboratories in this country, as well as in New Jersey USA and then lease them back as tenants. SHAC now has supporters in most European countries and also in the USA. Our groups continue to support the work of SHAC and I have no doubt that within my lifetime the HLS will close down.

Chapter Ten

A Cry from the Heart

"Animals are excited by the same emotions as ourselves. Terror acts in the same manner on them as it does on us, causing the muscles to tremble, the heart to palpate and the sphincter to be relaxed and the hair to stand on end."

Charles Darwin – The Descent of Man

I am sometimes asked why, when I retired from child protection work, I did not devote my remaining years to voluntary work with children and the agencies representing them. Intellectually, I could argue that children are protected by laws, although not always effectively, and the general public believe it is morally repugnant to abuse children, so the law and the force of public opinion are on their side. I do care about children and all vulnerable human beings and have always fought for them. My training as a nurse and social worker has equipped me well to do this, so I have been in many progressive movements such as introducing family planning to Pakistan; fighting for the rights of parents to visit and stay with their children in hospital; working with the victims of famine in India, and introducing a pioneering programme in Calcutta to reduce the maternal and infant death rate – but I sound defensive, as though I were making excuses for devoting the rest of my life to animals. I recognise that I have an intense concern and compassion for animals which, as I described earlier, may have derived from the companionship of the little cat that looked after me when I was a toddler left alone in the house by my violent mother. But this intensity of feeling, the heart rending empathy with suffering animals, is shared by all the activists I know. A friend told me that she grieved for her little dog who died recently "far more than I did when my mother and husband died". People tend to say

"I know I shouldn't be in such a state over an animal", but I am glad we are in touch with our feelings and honest about the depth of our love.

When I was older and could read, I was deeply influenced by Kipling and identified with Mother Wolf who cared for Mowgli. This makes it difficult for me not to embrace every German Shepherd I meet. However, I had a taste of reality when I was working in the eastern provinces of Turkey for the World Health Organisation, who wanted to start a national health service in those remote regions. We stayed in a derelict hospital and at night I could hear the wolves howling as they rummaged in the dustbins for food. An amazing sound, but I am not sure I wanted to live with them! The paediatrician with whom I was working carried a gun as we tramped across the snow fields to the remote villages. Tourists think of Turkey as a hot country, but in the eastern provinces the villages are covered in snow. The people live in one room with their cattle or sheep, waiting for the storks to return as harbingers of Spring.

In different circumstances, I suppose I should have trained for conservation work, but because I had no education I decided to train as a nurse, and managed to pass a general knowledge exam which qualified me to apply to St Thomas' Hospital and embark on four years training. But this feeling I have of Karmic affinity with animals continues – a feeling shared with thousands of other animal rights activists, and also, I think, with countless members of the public who ring me on my animal rights helpline, sometimes apologetic though less so nowadays, because they are grief-stricken at the death of a companion animal. I have many calls from the concerned public: for instance, a lady rang yesterday to tell me that a mother duck had elected to hatch fourteen babies in her shrubbery and what should she do? This morning another lady rang to ask what she should do about a traumatised mouse she had found in the kitchen. My answer: "Put him in the bathroom and treat for shock, then put him to bed with a little water". The stereotype of "animal lovers" used to be lonely spinsters, the elderly, the childless and other particularly needy souls, but I have considerable evidence to show that, for most people, the love of animals is universal. It is certainly instinctive in most children, except of course those who live on another planet, corrupted by greed and ignorance, who ignore or perpetuate abuse of our fellow creatures.

Those of us in the animal rights movement are called "nuts", "extremists", "terrorists", "fanatics" and "undesirable elements" on the one hand, and on the other we have been described as typically middle class, bunny-hugging middle-aged women "who might be seen shopping in Sainsbury's on any given day". I think we are united by an intense concern and wonder at the living world. My friend Molly, who is terminally ill with cancer, rang me last night to say that she had hung up her lace curtain to dry and when she went to fetch it she'd found a mother spider had laid a batch of eggs along the hem, so she cut off the hem and put the little family in the flower bed. I always check the plastic bin liners and pavements on dustbin day to collect the snails and put them in my window boxes and baskets, where I suppose is to be expected, they produce a lot of babies.

One of the most difficult emotions for us to deal with is our anger. It is hard for us to understand the many members of the public who are not so much guilty of culpable ignorance, i.e. they don't want to know, as a real lack of knowledge about animal abuse: "I never eat red meat, only fish and chicken", not realising there are nine-hundred million birds bred every year by the intensive poultry industry in this country, and that male baby chicks are separated from their mother at birth in the poultry units, thrown into sacks and suffocated because they cannot lay eggs and so are redundant to the food industry. I have written elsewhere about the fate of mother cow and her calves, living her entire life in grief and pain, and about the public misconception that animals in slaughterhouses are killed mercifully. People tell me "I don't mind eating meat as long as the animals are humanely killed". We often feel very helpless and frustrated, recognising that all animals reared for food are treated like slaves, their only value as a commodity. Fish, too, gasping for breath as they are dragged from seas and rivers or the stinking fish factory units. My warrior sister Fran's son, Jordan, aged four, seeing a man fishing on the banks of the river, left his mother's side as we were walking along the riverbank and said to the man, "You shouldn't do that, it's cruel to hurt a fish." The astonished fisherman said, "But don't you eat fish?". "Of course not, I'm a vegan," Jordan snapped back proudly. Fran congratulated him on making a stand. Jordan recognised that we blur issues by our inability to say something is wrong, recognising that although most abuse of animals is lawful it is still immoral.

Jordan

The public are unaware that animals suffer not only physical and emotional abuse but are also sexually abused by artificial insemination, such as the so-called 'rape racks' used for inseminating goats and other animals, and semen obtained from turkeys by masturbation. I do wonder who volunteers to do these jobs. I have tended to avoid the words sadistic cruelty, as I think most cruelty to humans and animals is not necessarily sadistic but due to ignorance and apathy. However, there is evidence of blatant sadism such as the terrible cruelty meted out to turkeys by a catching gang on a Bernard Matthews turkey unit filmed undercover by an investigator from Hillside animal sanctuary and shown on TV. The film showed the catchers kicking the turkeys for no purpose except to cause pain, throwing the terrified birds into the air and hitting them with poles. It is probable that this is just an example of what they do all the time. The poor victims would have arrived at the slaughter plant after a terrible road journey crammed in crates on trucks. One questions whether the 'official' veterinary surgeons are supposed to be on duty and alert to problems, but no one reported the inexplicable injuries to birds. Perhaps they do not care. The RSPCA has carried out a full investigation and has submitted a case file to their prosecution department. I have myself been inside several of Bernard Matthews' turkey farms; they are appalling beyond description with dead and dying birds littering the ammonia stinking floor.

Thinking about animal rights protesters, I would identify their strong sense of injustice, hatred of cruelty, and compassion for living creatures that are powerless to resist. Elizabeth Lewin wrote: "Because of what happened to me during the Holocaust; because I was once a victim while others were silent about my pain, I don't eat animals, and I don't wear animals. Every life is precious. Our silence must end. When I look into animals' eyes I see what I felt" (*Archangel*, Issue 29).

The public are more aware of the suffering of animals in laboratories than they are about factory farming. Some may be reassured by the constant claims of vivisectors in the UK who state that we have the highest standards and best legislation in the world and that no animal suffers unnecessarily. It is claimed that legislation to protect animals is strictly enforced, but to my knowledge there has not been one prosecution of a vivisector, despite the blatant cruelty repeatedly exposed by undercover investigators. The Home Office is responsible for appointing inspectors, but there are only thirty of these to monitor what goes on in two hundred and twenty seven research establishment and three million experiments annually. Then again, we know that most establishments are aware when the inspector is due to visit as their secretaries have been told to lay on coffee and biscuits!

Researchers intending to experiment on animals have to apply for a licence. The applications are assessed by overworked inspectors who, in theory, have to be satisfied that the potential gain to humanity outweighs the suffering of the animal. This assumes that we are justified in doing cruel experiments if human beings benefit, a highly unethical and offensive view. As Bernard Shaw once remarked to a vivisector who claimed that experiments on animals were a necessary evil: "If it's evil it cannot be necessary". The sheer volume of work means that applications cannot be properly scrutinised and it is up to the researcher to specify whether the suffering to the animal will be 'mild, moderate or substantial'. But we know many experiments classified as 'moderate' do indeed cause severe suffering. Given a licence, the tormentors can in effect do what they like to the poor creatures, including burning, poisoning and surgical mutilation – hideous cruelty which goes on secretly, as it does in countries which torture human beings. Undercover investigations have filmed dogs being punched, monkeys left uncared for overnight after intensive surgery and data being falsified. I could give endless examples of blatant cruelty, but even without the physical pain, we have the heart-breaking knowledge that animals in research laboratories are imprisoned for life, humiliated, stressed beyond belief and suffering acute fear. Human beings disabled by panic attacks may understand what animals suffer wherever they are incarcerated, fearing pain and death until the final betrayal when they are killed, by no means always humanely.

Rats and mice, who under normal conditions have lively characters and individual personalities, are regarded as of no value and scientists usually breed far too many for the intended experiment. These are then 'sacrificed' by having their head smashed or they may be gassed. A friend of mine, a technician, told me about the thousands of rodents who are killed unnecessarily or given to students to practise their 'skills' on. My friend, who loves animals but could not get round to leaving her job, tried to keep the mice and rats in their family groups as she recognised how close these social relationships are. She also tried to let them die without panic. My friend paid the price perhaps in her retirement for not leaving her job or exposing what went on and now lives her life as a recluse, consumed by guilt and suffering from auto-immune illnesses. But she does put food out for the local rats.

I think it unlikely that researchers suffer from guilt. We have no evidence that our long campaigns have had any effect on them. As we know, many treat the animals with contempt. I do not know how far they are motivated by greed, the need to advance their careers, or the knowledge that they are heavily subsidised by grants from pharmaceutical firms. Perhaps some of them really do believe their work is worth while, but if this is so they must use some schizoid psychological mechanism to split their feelings from their intellect as they observe the suffering of the animals. It seems to me that vivisection should be relegated to the dark ages. Again and again we read of human catastrophes from drugs which have been tested on animals. The pain killer Vioxx recently caused thousands of heart attacks in humans, but not in monkeys. There was also the terrible disaster that crippled the lives of volunteers in clinical trials when they were given monoclonal antibody TGN1412 which had such awful side effects, although there had been none in animals given five hundred times the normal dose. No wonder the public are becoming wary of taking prescribed drugs. I would not claim that no benefit has ever been gained from animal experiments, but the results could have been obtained without them. Whatever happened in the past, the future of testing drugs lies in modern technology and a huge reduction in the use of household and garden chemicals. We are now more conscious of poisoning the planet with our garden sprays and household chemicals, if not ourselves.

Chapter Eleven

Proposed Primate Laboratory, Girton, Cambridge.

"Animals are drowned, suffocated and starved to death; they have their limbs severed and their organs crushed: they are burnt, exposed to radiation, and used in experimental surgeries; they are shocked, raised in isolation, exposed to weapons of mass destruction, and rendered blind or paralysed; they are given heart attacks, ulcers, paralysis and seizures; they are forced to inhale tobacco smoke, drink alcohol, and ingest various drugs such as heroin and cocaine."

Tom Regan in *"How to Justify Violence in Terrorists or Freedom Fighters".*

Some years ago, there were rumours of a plan for the University of Cambridge to build a primate laboratory research institution. This was confirmed when I was telephoned from Girton College by an academic acquaintance telling me there was a planning application before South Cambridgeshire Council.

Pat and Sue went down to the council to get a photocopy of the plan, and after a rapid consultation we printed off hundreds of leaflets about the proposal. We named our campaign Xcape, Cambridge against Primate Experiments. Our Cambridge animal rights group then alerted all the other national organisations, printed petitions, and organised hundreds of letters of protest to be sent to the council. We were fortunate that the national organisation Animal Aid became involved and gave their unstinting backing to the campaign. Perhaps for the first time in history, a coalition was formed of six representatives from the six national organisations, including the British Union for the Abolition of Vivisection (BUAV), the National Anti-Vivisection Society (NAVS), People for the Ethical Treatment of Animals (PETA), the International Primate Protection League (IPPL) and Europeans for Medical Advancement.

The proposal for the centre was opposed by the local council, the police, and defenders of the green belt area. The police were concerned because they were well aware of our tactics on previous campaigns, particularly at Huntingdon Life Sciences. The buildings would have been at a junction of major roads, making it easy for animal rights protesters to block the roads, bringing the city to a standstill and potentially endangering life.

There was a public inquiry, chaired by a government inspector, which went on for weeks. We were fortunate in having compelling evidence from a number of scientists opposing the project, from American campaigners, and from the Buddhist organisation, the Amida Trust, who stressed the ethical objections. The government inspector ruled against the university application for a variety of reasons, including the fact that the university had declined to give any first hand medical evidence in support of the project. In spite of the inspector's well considered report, it was overruled by John Prescott, scientific advisor to the government, and the plan to start the building went ahead.

Our Cambridge animal rights groups, supported by national organisations, and activists from around the country, continued to work to overthrow the plan, keeping the media fully involved. Almost immediately after the inquiry, a small group of seasoned animal rights warriors including Mel and Robert spearheaded a new group: SPEAC (Stop Primate Experiments at Cambridge), sweeping our local group along with them and building on our groundwork. We organised local protests, marches, and various other forms of tactical civil disobedience. Soon after this, reading through the university publications, I learned that Regent House in the university had not been informed by the executive committee that the project was opposed by animal activists, nor had they understood its true costs, so they had agreed to the plan in virtual ignorance of what was involved. This helped to cast doubt on the whole proposal and the press reported on the strange financial happenings in our famous university.

Needless to say, the suffering that the animals would have experienced formed no part of the objections by the planning committee, and it is doubtful if any member of the council or the university was troubled by this. If they were, it was not reflected in any expressed views. We were delighted

From right, Pat, Joan, Sheila and Fran

to have SPEAC with us, and to use their extensive experience to organise marches and demonstrations, such as climbing the University Church tower to hang banners and generally causing mayhem. It is interesting to reflect that no one was arrested for this, as they certainly would have been if it had been in Oxford, where we are now campaigning.

It was around this time that we formed particularly close relationships with activists from Bedford, Sheila and Fran, and they were with us when we chained ourselves to the Senate House railings in time-honoured fashion. I learned that it is a good idea to bandage your wrists with thick tape, when you're doing a 'chain-in' or when you expect to be handcuffed, as handcuffs can bruise the skin.

We decided to interrupt the honorary degree ceremony, so early in the morning I hired my University gown and sat on a market bench. A policeman came up and said, "I trust you are not planning anything you shouldn't, Joan." "As if I would," I responded. In contrast to Oxford, where we have reason to believe that the police and university work hand in hand, Cambridge police are unlikely to interfere with demonstrations against the university, as they regard this as a matter to be dealt with by the proctors, the university's own law enforcement officers.

As the noble procession came from the Senate House, with the distinguished academics and other eminent people who had been given honorary degrees walking slowly down King's Parade in their glorious, colourful and traditional robes led by the Duke of Edinburgh, we began to liven up the proceedings. Two friends, one postgraduate law student and a forceful and imposing member of the Bedford group had donned monkey costumes. The dignified procession kept their composure as the monkeys danced alongside, banners were unfurled and with much shouting through megaphones: "Stop the Girton Laboratories!"

I slid into the procession with my banner and wearing my MA gown, walking alongside the Duke, who looked like an Easter Island granite statue. We stayed with the procession until they walked into Peterhouse college for the celebratory lunch. It is a matter of regret that we can no longer use such tactics in our battle against the horrendous plans to build a research laboratory in Oxford. In 2007, we attempted a modest protest, but this resulted in 16 arrests and considerable violence by the police. The court case went on for a year, causing serious disruption in the lives of those concerned but did not succeed. The police were severely criticised and the campaigners are claiming substantial compensation.

As it seemed that the project might still go ahead, we continued to organise events, pulling in supporters from across the country and abroad. SPEAC organised marches and demonstrations in the city. The poet Benjamin Zephaniah addressed a massive demonstration on Parker's Piece, and our American friends Pamelyn and Dr. Jerry Vlasak, a trauma surgeon, gave powerful speeches. This may be one of the reasons they are both now barred from returning to England, together with a number of other professional and academic militant warriors in the USA, as potential or actual political terrorists.

We began to think we might complete this campaign successfully, as we remembered a Buddhist advisor saying that it would not be difficult to bring this city to a standstill. So when SPEAC organised another demonstration outside the proposed site, we sat down and blocked the road. I did not sit down, because if I had I would not have been able to stand up again – arthritis poses mobility difficulties. So a friend and I held a banner across the road, in front of the sit-down, and the traffic began to pile up. A policeman came up and said, "Joan, I'm warning you to take that banner down." When I refused the final warning, I was escorted to the police van. I had not planned to be arrested as, unless there is a good reason, it is sometimes a waste of time for the person arrested and the other supporters. But on this occasion, acting on impulse, it seemed a good gesture to get publicity.

Down at the police station, my belongings were searched, and there were the usual procedures. Being arrested is still a relatively novel experience for me, as it had only happened on two previous occasions. Nowadays, of course, as the opposition becomes more formidable, activists are more routinely arrested, often without cause, and many are serving outrageously long prison sentences. Fortunately those who have been imprisoned come out again and rejoin the fray. At the station, the woman police officer put my belongings on the desk and arranged six stuffed toy mice in a row. "They're full of cannabis," I said. But then, not wanting them to be cut open or confiscated, I added, "But it's harmless, catnip gives cats a wonderful high." As is our custom, I pleaded not guilty, gave no information, and was locked in the cell. It can be quite boring, sitting in a cell for hours on end, though none of my warrior friends make any fuss about it. I find it okay provided I have a book, and I always carry one on demonstrations.

Being arrested, unless you are accustomed to it, is still no joke. You can be kept for hours in a 'paddywagon' with small concrete cells and you can either freeze to death or get very hot. If you are claustrophobic, it's a good idea to carry a herbal remedy. Should you want to do so, there is nowhere to pee. Useful advice to novice protesters going on a demonstration is "empty bladder and full stomach".

After some hours I was charged and released. I thought it would be possible to get a good deal of mileage for the campaign when the case came to court, using the argument, as anti-war protesters do, that my crime was committed to prevent a more serious one – to prevent a holocaust of primates. I would have been able to muster quite a formidable defence and a number of expert witnesses, but the case was dropped as "not in the public interest". There is no doubt that as a seasoned campaigner of advanced years I have always been treated with courtesy by the police, but I'm aware that many of my warrior friends have had appalling experiences at the time of arrest and in custody. I use my age as capital, that is, an asset which can be exploited.

The campaign ended when the University of Cambridge backed down and the application to build the centre was withdrawn. If it had been built it would have been the largest primate research laboratory in Europe. The abandonment of the project was widely reputed to be because of animal rights activists, but no doubt there were other financial considerations. I wish there was evidence that the university itself had any concern about the planned hideous experiments, which they had boasted would lead to advanced medical improvements in the treatment of people with degenerative diseases. All this was to have been heavily subsidised by the government, research organisations and the iniquitous pharmaceutical industry, so defeating the University of Cambridge was a great triumph.

Chapter Twelve

Moral Obligations to Animals

From their hearts of darkness and unredeemed consciousness, they dream up experiments that are as grotesque and cruel as they are without any commercial value to human health.

Anon

I am well aware that experiments on animals, including primates, continue in several departments of the university, and in the hospitals. The suffering of primates in Cambridge was exposed by a young girl working as an agent for the British Union for the Abolition of Vivisection who spent ten months undercover filming in a department that held primates. Her work was published in a documentary, *The Cutting Edge*, and in videos, and contained horrifying revelations of experiments on marmosets. Unlike other victims of violence – women and children, old people, the handicapped – non-human animals have little or no protection in law. Regarded as disposable objects, at the end of their lives in the laboratory they are dumped in black sacks marked 'disposable waste' and burned in incinerators. Each and every one of them is deprived of life and liberty and at the mercy of ruthless and/or ignorant so-called researchers. I recall Hilda shouting outside one institution, "We should bomb the bastards! If the bombs killed the animals, it would be a kinder fate than what they suffer at the hands of you lot!"

Doctor Vlasak, in an interview (*Arkangel*, issue 29) stated: "I think most humans have a sadistic strain, evidenced by the way they treat each other, not to mention non-human animals and the environment. The same ability to torture and kill concentration camp prisoners allows humans to continue torturing and killing animals today... The Nazi experiments are a good example; a lot of useful information came out of them. They are scientifically valid but immoral. In the case of animal experimentation, though, the vast majority of scientific research is invalid, as well as 100% immoral."

Sometimes animal rights protesters feel like aliens on the planet, or in a parallel universe. One of the fundamental difficulties is the gulf we feel between those who feel strongly that they have a moral obligation towards animals to be their advocates, and the rest of the world who eat them and make no connection between the living creature and the dead flesh on their plate.

Making the connection may come suddenly, or from a gradual realisation of the cruelty involved in the rearing and killing animals for food. One of the leading campaigners in a national organisation promoting veganism is a butcher's daughter, who as a young child ate meat without a thought. One day she was taken to a farm and met the living creatures for the first time – pigs, cows and chickens – and the full horror of their fate came to her with a blinding insight. She was terribly upset and instantly became a vegetarian, and later a vegan. Another fearless campaigner, Lyn Sawyer, a graduate midwife, was once an ardent hunter.

Most of us in the animal rights movement have been meat eaters in our time. I certainly was, until I came under the influence of Gandhi. But there have been many periods in my career when I simply forgot about it, or deliberately cheated, as I did when I was a student nurse during the war. As a vegetarian I was given a large allowance of cheese on my ration book, but this didn't stop me going to Lyons Corner House on my day off and eating steak and kidney pudding. Like many adults who come from an abusive background, I am greedy not just for food but for everything in life.

It is probably an oversimplification to think of people in general as callous and uncaring. Many are genuinely puzzled and ask, 'But what can we eat with our vegetables if we don't eat meat or fish? And how will we get enough calcium and protein?" Others, for whom I have little sympathy, just say "That is what animals are for." I'm not surprised that so few of us in the animal rights movement belong to an established church since we believe that the life of an animal is of equal value to that of a human.

Christians believe that human beings were made in the image of God and thus have a special place in the universe. Animals, if they could express their fear and panic, would be more liable to view us as agents of the Devil. There are philosophical arguments about desperate situations where one might choose to save the life of a human rather than an animal, and esoteric arguments are put forward to support this view. But we are more concerned with the day to day abuse of animals than with obscure dilemma such as whether if your boat was sinking you would save your dog or your child.

Not to be too cynical, there is no doubt that awareness is on the increase. Year after year our members give lectures to schools and colleges. Children, with their natural affinity for the living world, are often open to 'conversion' and frequently convert their parents. But we are still up against a massive ignorance about nutrition. Parents are naturally concerned that their children should be properly nourished. Fortunately there is now considerable literature to help parents understand the advantages of a plant-based diet for health, avoidance of obesity and reduction of serious illnesses in later life. Others like the opportunity to help save the planet and its resources. The march of so-called civilisation has had disastrous consequences on the health of many populations. In China, for example, people are now succumbing to diseases such as heart disease, high blood pressure and diabetes as they eat the junk food of the Western world and as meat replaces traditional soya-based products.

As the planet succumbs to global warming, water shortage due to the melting of the glaciers may well limit factory farming, but by then it will be too late. The devastation caused in the production of meat is graphically described by Juliet Gellatley in her ground-breaking book, The Silent Ark, which has done much to convert educated people to vegetarianism and veganism. As she argues, environmental collapse is accelerating, with the increasing degeneration of once fertile lands from livestock grazing. The deserts invade once verdant lands and a third of the world's surface rapidly becomes desert as the original soil breaks down, great rivers dry up and the poor are compelled to live in squalid slums that now surround all cities in the third world. It is always the poor who suffer from our greed. It looks as though Bangladesh, known as East Bengal when I worked in the beautiful villages of the Ganges, will finally die not from flooding, as has happened in the past, but from thirst as the waters vanish.

As the forests have been destroyed in the Amazon and elsewhere to clear the land for grazing cattle, carbon dioxide is released from the soil into the atmosphere and causes global warming. Gellatley notes that cattle belch and fart some 200 litres of methane every day which, added to the burning of vegetation, makes cattle grazing the second largest contribution to global warming after fossil fuel burning.

In the UK we are too complacent and think that the problems in the developing nations can't happen here in our so-called green and pleasant land. But our soil is poisoned by a frightening array of chemicals, nitrogen-based fertilisers and pesticides. How much this contributes to the alarming increase in cancer and other diseases we have little means of knowing. The macho culture of the USA particularly, which regards eating meat and especially beef as a mark of manhood, is making a massive contribution to the destruction of the world. Cows need cereals and water, and every kilogram of beef needs 3000 litres of water to produce as well as massive quantities of cereal. In the UK we are horrified that the sick desire for exotic meat has brought further exploitation of animals, with farmers now breeding crocodiles and ostriches for food. Far from the banks of the Zambezi or the Nile, the poor crocodiles are incarcerated in muddy tanks in a dark shed.

So a meat-based diet is helping to kill the planet. But I doubt whether the general public can take this in, and they are unlikely to do so until the flood waters invade our own sitting-rooms, and we have to queue up for drinking water from standpipes.

Chapter Thirteen

The Killing of So-Called Alien Species

In moments of helplessness and despair, we may ask whether the world is worth saving."

Lord Houghton of Sowerby

I do not believe we have the right to say which species should live and which should die. Animal Aid state that it is conservation hooligans who take it upon themselves to identify morally good and bad species, presuming to know the ideal population levels for each species, which results in ruthless and ignorant killing and a total disregard for the welfare of individual animals. The Grey Squirrel, for instance, introduced in the mid 19th century is still regarded as an invader, accused of taking up the space used by Red Squirrels, although it is humans that have played a major part in the Reds demise by destroying their natural habitat. The RSPCA also regards Grey Squirrels as vermin and will not treat them if injured. Fortunately we have other resources if we find one who that is sick or injured.

The RSPB also has strangely warped ideas and has called for a cull of the Ruddy Duck due to the fact that it is successfully breeding with our White Headed Duck. I think we were successful in stopping one of the Cambridge colleges slaughtering Canada Geese: they were using the excuse that the birds disturbed the students, though it was a student who alerted us to the proposed killing. There are also complaints that ducks and geese make a mess of college lawns and the river embankment, but human beings are in no position to complain about this natural littering! The RSPB are not consistent. The Brown Hare and the Little Owl are both foreign, but warmly welcomed. All this reminds one of ethnic cleansing and our own ambivalence towards immigrants.

There have been many complaints about activists releasing mink from mink farms. Actually it was farmers who first released mink into the wild, due to financial bankruptcy. Fortunately all fur farms in the UK were made illegal in 1998. The mink were classed as villains and their suffering while incarcerated was ignored. Released into the wild, hundreds were blasted by pheasant farmers to protect their own hideous trade.

I understand that mink often live a solitary life in the countryside and according to scientific studies have had no demonstrable impact on other species except the water vole. Our rivers are already in such an unhealthy state due to pollution that the voles are robbed of a healthy environment anyway. A BBC producer reported that "on a healthy well stocked waterway wildlife can co-exist, and there is a danger that mink can become a scapegoat to man's own damaging action on the river habitat". And so it goes on repeatedly: non-human animals are blamed for environmental disasters and endangering other creatures when it is actually human beings who bring about destruction through ignorance and greed. Another example is the blaming of badgers for giving TB to cows when it is more probably caused by cows being ruthlessly exploited to exhaustion and thus more likely to catch infection, and by the fact that the soil is depleted of minerals that could protect both cows and badgers from infection.

At the moment it is legal to kill certain species such as magpies, rooks and crows, but not others. The RSPB say that these species come under a special licence which they hope to challenge.

Chapter Fourteen

Blood Sports

There's no impersonal reason for regarding the interests of human beings as more important than those of animals.

Bertrand Russell.

From time to time we have attempted to interrupt and sabotage shoots, and we were successful in stopping John Lewis plc from giving their partners days out shooting pheasants. In Cambridge we engaged in street theatre, which I always enjoy, walking into John Lewis shops and giving out leaflets from Animal Aid and the League against Cruel Sports which revealed, for example, that the major shooting agri-businesses breed and release thirty-five million pheasants annually, half of whom perish from disease, exposure, malnutrition or under the wheels of motor vehicles. Of the sixteen million pheasants that are shot, it is estimated that just eight million are actually eaten. The others, who are wounded and not retrieved, die a lingering death. It was going out with my grandfather on one such a shoot when I was about ten and seeing the birds fall from the air that started me off as an animal activist, since I innately understood that it was cruel and wicked to harm an innocent bird. As we gave out leaflets in John Lewis, a group of us spread out a table cloth in the carpet department and set out a vegan meal which we proceeded to eat calmly as other campaigners regaled the public. As ever, we were asked to leave by the managers. We refused until the police were called and then left quietly as requested. We couldn't do this nowadays as we would be arrested for 'harassment' and interrupting a lawful business.

Sometimes, usually en route to a demonstration, we have seen farmers and others out shooting. The thing to do when this happens is to walk into the field in front of the guns while other activists try to chase the hares and rabbits out of the fields. This makes the farmers very cross and I think some of them are genuinely puzzled by our presence. When the police arrive, we leave but this has from time to time resulted in a summons. One time I remember attempting to chase the hares on to the adjoining golf course, but they seemed not to be golfing fans. One blessing is that hare coursing with dogs is now illegal and the police have been active in tracking down illegal hare coursers.

In August 1999, we heard that the Bishop of Bury St Edmunds was trying to raise money for a new church tower by giving donors an opportunity to go out on expensive shoots and hunts. We contacted Animal Aid, who organised a street theatre event. Cathedral staff came out to find us demonstrating a drama in which Jesus Christ in the person of a tall, granite faced campaigner, dressed in white, was dying for the animal victims. The Dean came out and said "This can't go on", as they did not want the bad publicity, particularly as we threatened to go on hunger strike if the plans went ahead. Subsequently these prizes were withdrawn, not out of principle but out of fear of a bad press. A woman priest from the cathedral complained to me that the play was "sacrilege" and I responded by telling her that I thought the killing of animals for pleasure was repugnant, that if Jesus were here he would condemn it and that she should take a leaf from the Vicar of Dibley. She walked away looking rather cross.

Although hunting with dogs is illegal, we continue to monitor hunts as the hunters do all they can to find loopholes in the law so that they can continue to enjoy their bloodthirsty 'sport'. City foxes abound and my garden fox enjoys a good diet, particularly relishing Christmas puddings that were surplus to my own requirements. Several excellent organisations, including The Fox Project, specialise in rescuing foxes, treating their ailments and injuries and rehabilitating them. Nevertheless, foxes are still persecuted and the police are reluctant to take action against those who infringe the law.

Unfortunately, fishing is not generally regarded as cruel. Scouts and others involved in youth activities encourage fishing competitions, though the scout law states: "A Scout knows there is strength in being gentle... he does not harm or kill any living thing". Anglers argue that fishing is a sport enjoyed by thousands of people, including the monarchy. Well, members of the royal family are not known for their compassion towards animals, happy to slaughter harmless birds on massive and murderous shoots, to wear fur, and to support horse racing with its annual toll of death and disease as exhausted horses succumb to stress disorders and may well end their days in horsemeat markets.

To return to fishing, we have campaigned against it by disturbing the water where people are fishing and informing the public about the cruelty involved. Fish hauled from the water suffocate as their gills collapse. Even if they are returned to the water, their skins are damaged. The RSPCA sponsored a three-year investigation which concluded fish are indeed capable of experiencing pain and suffering, and in 1996 DEFRA came to the same conclusion. As for fish farming, poor salmon are deprived of the experience of swimming up-river and fulfilling their instinctive behaviour.

People who continue to fish claim that they help to keep rivers clean, but this task is effectively carried out by the RSPB, the Environment Agency and British Waterways even during the close season when the anglers leave. Fishing also causes pain and suffering to other species. Between 1995 and 1997 the RSPCA wildlife centre treated 1,491 mute swans suffering from ingesting lead fishing weights and tackle. Many die painfully. In the same period, there were 230 other victims of fishing lines – ducks, geese, moorhens, hedgehogs, coots, and more. I have a friend who became a vegan, vowing never to eat fish again after she nearly drowned and experienced the terror of suffocating.

Fish farms are overcrowded – as many as 5000 salmon may be kept in one sea cage, making them likely to be diseased with parasites, sea lice and pancreatic disease. According to the Animal Aid publication, *The Fishing Industry 2006*, lice infestation is devastating and may eat the fish alive. The fish are regularly dosed with chemicals and antibiotics. But between 20 and 50 per cent still die of pancreatic cancer or kidney infections. Like other factory farmed creatures, farmed fish are genetically modified to make them grow fatter and bigger, which causes deformities and much suffering.

Fish caught at sea have no legal protection and their fate has been vividly described in the reports of Sea Shepherd, who campaign against the vast drag nets. The fish come up from the deep and experience excruciating decompression, causing ruptures, and gasping for air so that their eyeballs pop out. Fortunately, the Dutch – unlike the British – are looking into the fish industry slaughter methods, which may result in new animal welfare legislation. To date, fish have no legal protection. Nor do those who eat fish, unaware of the danger of mercury poisoning. Non-oily fish may be contaminated with toxins, and pregnant women are advised by the medical authorities to limit the amount of tinned tuna that they eat. I can't think who would want to eat fish that are likely to contain so many contaminants as well as sea lice!

Chapter Fifteen

More of Hilda

The fate of helpless animals is of more importance to me than the fear of appearing ridiculous.

Emile Zola

Hilda's health began to be of concern to me in 1997, after I had ceased work and we were able to spend more time together. When I was away she would take care of my cats and in exchange I cooked for her. She was still riding her bright red tricycle and was a menace on the roads, seldom making hand signals.

Hilda liked to go to the market to pick up cabbage leaves for my rabbits. "Why waste money buying greens", she would say. We would pick up other discarded vegetables dropped under the stalls and stop to swear at the fish merchants when they sold live lobsters. Once we brought a poor living creature and took her to the sea at King's Lynn. I did not know at the time that the practice of buying live animals at the market and then releasing them as an act of compassion is known as *Hojo* and is a widely practiced Buddhist ritual in other countries. Sadly, this leads to further trauma, especially to wild birds caught and trapped specifically for this ritual, thus making money for the market dealers. Perhaps we had better stick to releasing lobsters!

Hilda, if she were still alive, would be glad to know about the Lobster Liberation Front, who specialise in destroying lobster pots, and also the Shellfish Network, which exposes cruelty to all crustaceans. These specialist groups, usually established by one person with a burning concern who becomes a specialist in the field, are enormously important, amassing scientific evidence in an attempt to convince politicians that these creatures feel pain.

Regrettably the public may be unmoved by compassion when they see packaged bits of animals in the shops, but exposés on television do make an impact, which we can then follow up by producing our own material. For instance, Hillside animal sanctuary recently exposed the disgusting conditions in RSPCA Freedom Food duck factory farms. Why the RSPCA ever embarked on sponsoring so-called Freedom Foods is a mystery to me. They would argue that since people eat meat, the condition of factory farms needs to be improved. But the label Freedom Foods is misleading. The RSPCA claim that they are not a vegetarian society. I can't think why not, since their purpose is to encourage kindness to animals. But moving the RSPCA into the 21st century is a hard task. Many of us remain members because of the RSPCA's great influence in Parliament and the heroic work often done at a local level by regional groups acting as independent charities. However, I continue to hope that the RSPCA will become more radical and enlightened, and will succeed, as the NSPCC has done, in changing their ways whilst still remaining a useful political force. I worked for the NSPCC for five years, and I can claim some credit for its rebirth as a truly professional body. The most powerful impetus for change is when an organisation loses money and support.

Hilda was by then 84 and increasingly frail. In spite of this, she still loved her trips to London, which she saw through Dickensian eyes, with the streets full of gangsters and murderers. But she also loved wandering down the King's Road, feeding the pigeons regardless of the notice instructing people not to, buying soap at Lush and as happy to be with me as I was to be with her. Best of all she enjoyed the Notting Hill Carnival, caught up by the Caribbean dancing and joining in the gaiety and noise.

Hilda was in her element too at Reclaim the Streets demonstrations, laughing at the police trying to block the road. "Oh look, a naked man," she said, observing one who was jumping about on top of a taxi. But at home I noticed she needed to sit down more frequently, glad of the seats kindly supplied at Marks and Spencer's. Her pulse was irregular, so I arranged for her to see a GP, who referred her to a cardiologist. She was prescribed various medicines, which she found confusing, and complained of some abdominal pain, for which she was given pain killers which did not help. "Something is wrong,' she said grimly, suspecting that she had been misdiagnosed. She lost weight rapidly, but neither her GP nor the hospital considered the possibility that her cancer might have recurred. It was now five years since her original operation for colonic cancer. Three days before she died, I took her to the hospital and pointed out her symptoms. The consultant said "We will look into all that once we have successfully treated her heart condition." She complained of constipation and was prescribed Senna, which probably caused her gut to perforate, leading to peritonitis and septicaemia. Two nights before she died, Hilda stayed the night at my house, complaining of appalling abdominal pain. The GP came out reluctantly, but when she saw how Hilda was suffering she sent for an ambulance. Fortunately I had one morphia tablet which I had acquired from a friendly dying friend and had kept for emergencies. I gave it to Hilda. "Swallow this", I said, knowing it was unlikely she would be given pain relief in hospital before she saw a consultant. I only wish I could have put her to sleep, as I would a loved and dying companion animal. She was subjected to the usual scans and x-rays in an attempt to discover the source of internal bleeding until, reflecting her wishes, I insisted they stop. I stayed with her for the last two nights, trying to make her as comfortable as possible, and in spite of the notice saying nil by mouth I persuaded the medical staff to allow her to have a drink of water, as it could make no difference to her condition. The nurses were efficient and kind, and willing to call the doctors when it was obvious that Hilda needed higher doses of morphine. She drifted into unconsciousness without a word and died peacefully at dawn. Ken had told me to call anytime, and I did. We went home together.

I saw no need to rush Hilda's funeral. She had been frightened of being either buried or cremated, which rather restricted our choice. "I'm afraid to be buried alive', she said. So I put off the cremation for fifteen days, which gave me time to write to all her animal rights friends. We planned a send-off worthy of a cockney gangster, which she would have loved. Minus the funeral plumed black horses, as this would have been too expensive. Instead we took the coffin in a local wildlife ambulance, flying purple ribbons and flags, and decorated her house with purple blossoms and hanging baskets. I told the police we were going to hold up the traffic; as Hilda had always done this it came as no surprise. We drove up and down Mill Road, reversing and going back again, to allow her shopkeeper friends to see her go by. Other passers-by thought our cortège was some sort of festival, as indeed it was, celebrating her life as a unique human being. Her coffin was carried by four of her young animal rights friends, who decided to wear suits for the occasion: "I don't think I know how to fix a tie", lamented Darren.

The service caused some anxiety to the staff, who remarked, "We have never seen anything like this", as animal rights campaigners filled the room. Michael Sutcliffe, looking very respectable, conducted the service, which had a formal structure but included many impromptu speeches. We sang *Bright Eyes* and ended with *Jerusalem*, which would have delighted Hilda. As her coffin, decorated with a beautiful cloth and hundreds of badges, slowly disappeared, John Curtin stood up and cried, "What do we want?' "Animal Rights!" we responded. "When do we want it?" "Now!" It was a moving and theatrical event, in tune with Hilda's wonderful *joie de vivre*. We later celebrated with a vegan meal and Pat put on an exhibition of press cuttings and photographs illustrating Hilda's life's work. I thought, "It's annoying she can't come home and celebrate with me yet another animal rights event." Even now, a decade later, I dream that Hilda has died and wake up desolate to find that it is true. Friendship has always been central to my life. And Hilda had special qualities that were recognised by many people. Her neighbour Anne said, "I still hear the sound of Hilda calling home her cats. She had a rare quality of making you feel safe."

I kept Hilda's ashes on the sideboard. Ken took some to Kenya, in memory of our several safaris, remembering how Hilda stood up on a truck where a pride of lions were devouring their prey, shouting, "That lion has an injured paw!" "And you'll be killed dead", said the warden, pushing her back in her seat. The lion snarled at us and the warden assured Hilda that he would come out to treat the lion.

I also use Hilda's ashes for pet graves, and will keep some to mix with mine when I go. On one notable occasion John Curtin threw a handful of ashes into the air over the entrance to Huntingdon Life Sciences one moonlit night and they rained down spectacularly. There must be something deep in our psyches that fuels these rituals and brings some comfort to mourners, recognising the respect that we have for the deceased and ensuring the safe passage of souls.

Most people I know bury their pets with great ceremony, wrapping them in blankets, covering their eyes with flower petals, burning a candle in their memory. Those who consider this sentimental underestimate the intensity some people feel for their companion animals, and also the importance of ritual. Our animal companions are indeed our solace, as we sleepwalk though a nightmare world. As Michel de Montaigne wrote, "With regard to friendship, that of animals is without comparison. More compassionate and constant than that of man."

Many people have been betrayed and disillusioned by the human race and it is inevitable that as individuals we will find consolation in our companion animals. I am fortunate that my trust in friends and lovers has not been seriously eroded. My non-human friends are, of course, utterly incapable of letting me down. We are their world, they are ours. And our mutual devotion is woven into the fabric of our lives.

Chapter Sixteen

Sea Shepherd

Begin each morning by saying "People are a mistake".
Quentin Crisp

In July 2004 I set out for Brazil as a newly recruited crew member of the Sea Shepherd flagship the *Farley Mowat*. How did this come about? I met the American trauma surgeon Jerry Vlasak, and his wife Pamelyn when they came to give evidence at the Cambridge inquiry in opposition to the proposed vivisection laboratory at Girton. Later, over a gin and tonic, Jerry noticed my Sea Shepherd sticker and told me he was a director of the Sea Shepherd Conservation Society.

Pamelyn is a trained nurse who met Jerry and fell in love watching him calmly dealing with a victim suffering a blasted gunshot wound to his face. Jerry radiates a powerful and contained energy and I was not surprised to hear that during the bloody seal cull, stranded on moving ice and needing to get back to our ship, he stopped to shield a photographer from a deranged sealer, taking the blow from the axe on his own face. He was promptly arrested for attempting to disrupt the cull, handcuffed and left all night on deck. He later faced fines for his unlawful activity which he refused to pay and went on a fifteen-day hunger strike while in prison. He is now a press officer for the North American Animal Liberation Front.

As we drank our gin and tonic, I said to Jerry, "If only I were fifty years younger, I could volunteer as crew". "Come," he said, "We will pay to renew your subscription if you fill in the application form." I owe him a great debt for enabling me to enlist as a crew member.

I had long been an admirer of Captain Paul Watson, reading his log and bulletins and his gripping book, *Ocean Warrior*; with his account of twenty long years challenging illegal whale killers and fishermen, hauling up the long lines and driftnets heaving with their poor victims caught on the hooks – turtles, dolphins, tuna and every kind of pelagic creature swept up in these murderous destroyers of the ocean.

Captain Paul Watson and his crew are famous for challenging Japanese whalers and Paul described his 'moment of truth' when, alone in a dinghy overshadowed by the huge whaling ship towering above him, a dying harpooned whale rose in the water above him, blood pouring from his wounds into the sea and engulfing Paul in his blood, who thought this was his last moment. The whale could have sunk the boat with his great weight. Paul saw his reflection in the creature's eyes in a second of mutual understanding, and then the whale flung himself away from the boat and sank beneath the waves.

Paul is a heroic figure, Churchillian in character, a former director of Greenpeace who established the Sea Shepherd Conservation Society in 1977 because of disagreements on tactics. Since then he has been sailing into harm's way with voluntary crews.

Direct action has always appealed to me and I have not found that advancing age has lessened the strong urge for adventure, so I telephoned Sea Shepherd's headquarters and spoke with Paul's wife Allison, known to the Japanese as a sea goddess and a redoubtable enemy of the Japanese since she released the dolphins in Taaji. I told her that I was probably too old and incapacitated, that I could not hear or see well and had arthritis, so I did not think her husband would consider me a suitable crew member. But she told me: "He's not like that" and went off to speak with him. And so began the great adventure, my mind full of dreams of raging seas, storms, and distant shores, as I made preparations to join the *Farley Mowat* on its Icelandic campaign to challenge the whalers.

No amount of heavy doses of reality, a lifetime of plunging into dangerous jobs and campaigns which inevitably involve loneliness, home sickness and physical discomfort, illness and fear, has curbed my lust for adventure. I remember recovering from a dangerous tropical illness in Calcutta, where I worked as a midwife in 1946, and coming to the end of my contract, reading an article in the *Nursing Times* about the Frontier Nursing Service in Kentucky, a horseback nursing service to the mountain people there. The fact that I could not ride or drive and had never worked outside a city did not deter me, and they offered me a contract. I sometimes wonder who is living my life and impelling me to invest such passion and energy into realising dreams. The igniting spark always arises from something I have read and I blame Rudyard Kipling for starting it all, as without the *Jungle Books* would I have volunteered to go to India? Among these dreams I weave Utopian aspirations with hopes of alleviating suffering in sentient beings. Fortunately my guardian angel is practical, so I have qualifications in nursing, midwifery and social work, and have climbed steadily up the education ladder from the time when I left school at twelve. I recognise that I live in my head and imagination, that I am impelled to take on enterprises and campaigns that call my soul to get my wits together and do something about it. For the last twenty-seven years it has been the call of the non-human world, the suffering of sentient beings that fills my heart with pity, anger and desolation.

To return to Sea Shepherd, with my mind full of Northern seas I began to collect suitable clothes as I knew it would be cold and wet to a degree I could hardly imagine. I spoke to Darren, a valued animal rights colleague with whom I'd been on many campaigns. "Come with me", I urged him, "Think of being with Captain Watson, and anyway I can't face travelling on my own, airports confuse me." "You're taking me into deep water", Darren remarked, but he agreed to come. He has been travelling and campaigning with Sea Shepherd ever since.

The voyage to Iceland was cancelled as Sea Shepherd could not put its limited resources into a campaign which seemed unlikely to achieve much. Instead, we were told to go to Brazil to join the crew sailing down the South Atlantic coast, searching out illegal fishermen and supporting local conservationists who were attempting to clear the coast of pollution. Darren and I set off for Curacao as approved crew members, complete with headlamps, heavy duty gloves to be used when scraping off barnacles, deck shoes and sun cream, but with very little vision of just how hot it was going to be. I was not particularly anxious as on the whole I am accustomed to feeling the same degree of apprehension on every enterprise, whether I am giving a dinner party or setting out on the high seas. But it was exciting to be on the way to our fabled ship.

We found the *Farley Mowat* rocking darkly in the harbour, flying the Canadian flag at its rear and the skull and cross bones at its fore. The *Farley Mowat* is a 677-ton Norwegian trawler, fifty metres long and fifty years old, battle scarred and in constant need of repairs. I am phobic about crossing gangways and the chief mate had not yet put up a handrail. Poor Darren, who is physically fearless, had to encourage me to cross the great divide over the harbour water, all five foot of it. Ridiculous! I find it hard to believe I once crossed the long swinging bridges in Kentucky. You have to work on phobias or they recur.

We were greeted by Alex, the chief mate, who looks remarkably like the singer Sting, and Adrian the second mate, an ex-treehugger from the Oregon campaign to save the Spotted Owl from the loggers. We were offered tea and shown to our cabins, the size of a small kitchen in a terraced house with two bunks, a hand basin, and a small rickety cupboard. I soon discovered that there was no real plumbing when I flooded the kitchen by not noticing that the sink drained into buckets, as did the basin in my cabin. The first night was traumatic as I had little sense of direction and could not find the lavatory, and we were plunged into complete darkness. We were always being plunged into darkness. But morning came and I found my way around the beautiful ship. The interior is decorated with murals of dolphins, whales and other sea creatures in brilliant colours. There are shields hanging from the walls which crew grab if they are attacked. On deck, there were three zodiacs, motorised dinghies, and a cannon which on at least one occasion fired custard pies and jellies on to indignant Japanese whalers!

We spent some weeks in harbour before setting sail as there is a great deal of work to be done in preparation for every campaign: tons of oil and water to be pumped, food to be collected from generous donors and stored, the ship thoroughly cleaned and painted, rust and barnacles chipped off and, not least, crew to be recruited. We slept on deck in harbour and as we sailed down the Brazilian coast Darren was cradled in a hammock. Alex told me, "I can always find work for anyone", so I helped in the kitchen, washing up, and took my turn on the bridge, dominated by gadgets of every description and a statue of the Tibetan Buddhists' wrathful deity Heruka, donated by the Dalai Lama when he blessed our ship.

We eventually set off, the gangway and anchor winched on board. It was pitch dark, there was a rough sea and I was overcome by panic and an acute sense of anxiety, "I can't get back", as land receded. So I did what I always do in psychic emergencies and withdrew with a book. Rocking on the narrow bunk, torch clasped in my hand, I took refuge in *Anna Karenina* and was soon engulfed in the snows of Russia.

Alex had told us never to undress completely and to leave our shoes ready, as "It only takes forty-eight seconds for a boat to sink". So last thing, I always put my bifocals carefully into my shoes. Neither Darren nor I were seasick. Darren stated that it was all in the mind, which clearly it was not, but we were lucky and in the morning I was elated to be on board mixing pancakes with Alex who, among his other talents (deep sea diver, inspiring chief mate) is also a splendid cook. Meals are very important to seamen, as we did twelve-hour shifts on the bridge among other duties, and the engineering staff are always starving and usually dehydrated, making frequent trips to the water barrels.

I took my turn on the bridge, learning to watch for long liners and ships on the horizon. It did not take long for me to realise that I did not understand how to chart and I was slow to learn how to use the instruments. Alex was patience itself and although I never became confident with technology, it was wonderful to see it all in action. I made friends with Graham, the third engineer, who has an encyclopaedic knowledge of sea life and regaled me with stories of their recent expedition to the Galapagos, where they were attacked by and taken hostage by Ecuadorian fishermen, angry at the crew's attempts to stop illegal fishing. The crew also spent their spare time arranging for the cats on the island to be neutered as otherwise they destroyed the local fauna. Graham taught me everything I now know about the state of the oceans. He was also immensely kind, fixing up a gigantic fan in my cabin, which was life saving as the temperature was usually around a hundred degrees Fahrenheit. In spite of the heat, we watched videos in the mess, a particular favourite being *Fawlty Towers*. I also made friends with the chief engineer, a Brazilian named Marino, the only paid member of our crew. He bore a surprising resemblance to Monsieur Poirot, down to the moustache he constantly adjusted. He spoke practically no English, but by sign language I discovered he had seven children, five of them engineers! "I make all work", he said and, "You are my mother", as he showed me his amulet containing a photo of his mother. His great muscular hand would grasp mine, appearing from nowhere whenever I crossed over a step to the deck. From time to time he came to where I was reading a book, exhausted from the heat, to give me a coconut into which he had tipped a generous amount of brandy. "Now you drink for health", he would say.

Graham flag waving on board the Farley Mowat

Quite early on when I was on bridge duty, I was sad to find I had lost my night vision and could not see the beautiful southern skies that I remembered so well from star gazing on the great P&O ocean ships en route to India. So my bridge duty was confined to daylight, and finished once I had switched on the navigation lights. On one occasion, unfortunately, I switched on the emergency lights which caused some consternation!

We had many delays on this campaign because the Brazilian authorities decided to make life difficult for our American crew members. As a result of the time lost, our captain had to curtail the campaign and I never got to hear the song of the humpback whales. Bea, a beautiful Brazilian girl with whom Graham fell in love, is studying the songs of the humpback whales and told me that the males changed their songs every three years to become more attractive to the females, who spend two years in Brazilian waters during pregnancy and childbirth before heading back out to the Antarctic. Our task there would have been to guard the nurseries against human predators. The curtailment was disappointing, but we had the joy of watching the spinning dolphins at Fernando de Noronha. We turned off the zodiac engine and cruised silently with them as they headed towards their fishing grounds. It was beautiful. And green turtles swam by, returning to their sanctuary on the north side of the island.

It was an achievement to learn how to go down a rope ladder into the zodiac, helped by willing hands, but once down it was exhilarating to speed among the islands. Although this island was a sanctuary, there were only a few coastguards to defend it from the illegal fishermen. One night we were alerted by the coastguards that illegal fishermen had been spotted on the south side of the island. It was a stormy night and plunging through rough seas with the wind howling like demented furies, the ship in darkness so we could advance unseen, I thought it best to retire to the captain's cabin, which he had allocated to me so that I could take care of the kitten he had rescued in an Amazonian port while he was in America on a lecture tour.

Cradling the kitten, named Itarqui, I tried to reassure her and myself that dawn would come and our plunging and rolling ship would return to calm waters. It was a long night which I found quite scary, probably because I was not on the bridge where I would have revelled in the excitement. But I was glad to be with Itarqui who bravely clung to my neck, her claws in my hair. She was terrified and so was I. The fridge blew open. Unlike every other item on board it was not roped up and anchored to the floor, so with a mighty crash it disgorged its contents: large jars of peanut butter, cat food, and jam. We can't do anything about it till dawn, I told Itarqui, who by this time had added to the chaos by being sick and tipping the litter tray of Galapagos sand all over the floor. At dawn I looked at the damage, but it was not so extensive and order was soon restored and Itarqui happily eating her breakfast.

When the captain returned he would take her up to the bridge where she would explore the compass, radar and other mysterious toys with delicate claws. She was much loved and Eduardo, a vet and one of the Brazilian crew, was her medical adviser, though he actually got her sex wrong as she turned out to be a boy. It was good to have Eduardo on board. He was a passionate anti-vivisectionist and had managed to complete his veterinary studies without having done any experiments on animals. Like all our Brazilian crew, he was heavily decorated with tattoos, including a tattoo of his beloved dog on his leg. As we had no doctor on board, it was reassuring to have a vet. Although I have a nursing background, my skills are very rusty and the thought of having to sew up any wounds filled me with dismay. "No problem", Eduardo reassured me as we rummaged through our medical room, which had once been tidy and well ordered but had never quite recovered from the inspection by the environmental officers who came on board and cast out most of our supplies that seemed to be out of date. I'm surprised they did not include the bandages, but we lost our rehydration packets – no great loss as I simply gave water with a pinch of salt and sugar to anyone dehydrated, or when one of our crew suffered from food poisoning. So in our medical supplies we were left with a mountain of sea sick remedies, antibiotics and a box mysteriously labelled "for boys and girls". Unfortunately for me, Eduardo was recruited in Brazil to take up a job as a conservation officer so, apart from myself, there was no one left on board with any medical knowledge. Although it was possible to send a satellite message to Jerry Vlasak in the USA (I did so on occasion when I could not work out the dosage on antibiotics), I felt uneasy. Luckily, after Eduardo left there was only one serious emergency when one of the engineers tripped over, falling heavily on pipes. "I think I may have cracked my ribs," he said casually, but as breathing did not cause him pain and he was not coughing blood I assumed he was only suffering severe bruising and prescribed pain killers. He recovered in a few days.

In general no members of the crew complained of minor illnesses or pain but would help themselves to any pills they thought they needed. The captain was well known for his impatience with "wimps and whiners", so crew members always said they were fine even when it wasn't true.

After our Brazilian crew left, leaving us with a heavily depleted crew, Darren was in his element taking on all the extra tasks with good humour and energy. Alex said, "I hope you can both rejoin the ship before we head for the Grand Banks and beyond", but by then we had decided to return home. We had been away for ten weeks. Darren had to sort out domestic affairs and I wanted to be back to rejoin the animal rights campaign and be reunited with my cats. At the end of my time on board, I remarked to Ken, my second adopted brother, that it was good to be back with all our normal neurotic friends. My beautiful Itarqui was taken by the captain to live in his home in Friday Harbour, near Seattle, to become another beloved pet for Allison. She sent me a photograph of him lying in splendour on the sofa, now sleek and big like a black panther, no longer a clinging little kitten. I miss him.

Our return journey was not without incident. One night the radar failed, then the automatic pilot, and then there was a small fire in the kitchen. I was never apprehensive about our safety as I had total confidence in the skills of the captain and chief mate, but I am concerned that the Sea Shepherd organisation has to manage on a shoestring and cannot afford essential repairs such as rewiring and plumbing. Following a recent campaign, there was also damage to the anchor chain, leakages and flooding. The organisation had a fundraising campaign to buy a new vessel, and have now been able to buy a faster ship which can keep up with the Japanese whalers and sabotage their dreadful trade.

Although life on board was not always easy, I remember wonderful long days on the bridge, despite seeing very few whales and dolphins at sea as their numbers have been so decimated. What we did see was all too visible: endless plastic bottles thrown overboard by freighters and cruise vessels, adding to the rubbish and poisons being churned out by the Amazon and other rivers. The oceans are ravaged, poisoned and destroyed by fishing, deliberate slaughter by whaling nations and dolphin and tuna killers. The food supplies of most ocean species have been plundered, the mangrove swamps destroyed by prawn fishing, and so it goes on. I know we must save what we can and am a wholehearted supporter of Sea Shepherd and their commitment to direct action, but the knowledge that the skies, earth and seas are poisoned makes one very doubtful the planet can survive. As Chomsky once wrote: "The human race is a biological error that inflicts calculated savagery on all other species."

Chapter Seventeen

Oxford

I left England to join the Sea Shepherd Conservation Society ship, the *Farley Mowat*, the day after I had completed a forty-eight hour fast under the holly tree on the site of the proposed laboratory. The ominous cranes were standing like giant dinosaurs about to plunge on to the concrete pillars and workmen were coming in and out. To date there is no law to prevent fasts and hunger strikes and because of the influence of Gandhi on my life, I have always thought that fasting is a non-violent and tactical way of legitimate protesting. My first fast in March 2004 was sponsored by and raised money for SPEAC (Stop Primate Experiments At Cambridge), who were surprised and pleased that the fast galvanised the local press (who until then had not reported any of the demonstrations) into giving a surprising amount of publicity. Soon after this, work on the building site in Oxford ceased and did not resume until November 2005, seventeen months later.

I staged a further hunger strike (seventy-two hours) in April 2005, carefully arranged by Mel and Robert of SPEAK, who organised that I should sit in Oxford outside St. Michael's church. Impractical as ever, I had expected the weather to be benign in April. It was not, and although Steve had arranged for me to sleep in his van at night I was very cold. I was well looked after by animal rights friends and always accompanied by a Buddhist friend, the Reverend Susthama, who woke me in the morning and I staggered out from the van. We walked from the van to the Randolph hotel, where no one stopped me using the luxurious facilities which included a warm loo seat in the disabled lavatory. Emerging clean and fresh, I rejoined Susthama in the lounge where we drank our hot water. I had no particular difficulty in going without food, but I could have been defeated by the cold. The hunger strike raised a substantial amount of money and publicity and is obviously a tactic to be considered in the future.

Joan on hunger strike

Joan and Rev. Susthama

Chapter Eighteen

My Fictive Family

If you're a snail it's a slow procedure. God doesn't promise too much to feed on if you're a snail. It's a great advantage to live in a garden with decent plantage.

Peter Levi.

There are advantages to having a biological family. With any luck your children look after you when you're old and your grandchildren think you're wonderful. I do not have a biological family. My father died when I was thirteen and my mother about thirty years ago.

My brother Peter, on whom I depended, was two years older than me and died two years ago – still at his computer. I was very emotionally dependent on Peter as when he was around order returned, and of course I believed he knew everything and would take charge. But at the age of six he was sent to prep school and then on to public school as my mother claimed he was unmanageable. As a small child I used to listen to his stories of school life, not understanding a word he was saying but identifying with him with that attentive manner I have cultivated so well even when I do not understand what is being said. In a Japanese prisoner of war camp, Peter later remarked that if you can survive boarding school a Japanese war camp poses no particular difficulties. Being a survivor like me, he adapted to work in the kitchens and learned Japanese. I met him in Bombay soon after he came out of prison. He had been held by the Japanese for seven years and looked skeletal from the effects of beriberi, but with his usual aplomb he escorted me through customs to the nearest European club for a gin and tonic and booked me into the Taj Mahal hotel – highly inappropriate, as I was about to join a Quaker unit who went in for simple living, but that was Peter. Later that night I left the hotel and walked around the back streets of Bombay to see how people really lived and as a gesture of solidarity put a five rupee note in the hands of a sleeping beggar.

Peter went on to marry several times, unfortunately at one stage concurrently, but he managed to convince Judge Mishkin that it was an error. The judge said this was not the behaviour of an officer and a gentleman, at which point I had difficulty controlling my hilarity, but subsequently I named one of my favourite cats Mishkin as I was grateful to the judge for not imposing any penalty on Peter. Peter went on to live happily with his third wife, a South American lady, in Argentina. As I have recounted elsewhere, Peter could not work in England as it gave him terrible panic attacks. During one of these in Marylebone Road, near the flat we had lived in with mother, he asked what had happened to us as children. I gave him some brief account and then referred him to a psychiatrist. He recovered and went back to South America. Although I was very dependent on Peter as a child, I was also extremely defensive and tried to protect him from our mother's brutality, not always successfully.

I am more fortunate than Peter was, as I have not repressed my memory of life as it was in our lonely childhood. Repressed memories tend to erupt like volcanoes giving rise to neurotic symptoms. Children living with an alcoholic parent may often be in a double bind - I knew with mother that if she saw me through her drunken rage she would attack, but on the other hand I did not like being quiet and invisible. This has left me with one major difficulty - a constant need to be known and recognised.

My 'fictive' family is my community of friends, a relationship bound together through our shared vision of the world in one way or another, similar to the Buddhist *sangha*, and a refuge from the great killer, loneliness. We are social animals, as are most living creatures, and this need was well fulfilled in my long professional life. It is really only since I retired more than a decade ago, at the age of seventy-seven, that I have sought ways to fill the gap. So I suppose in a reflection of Peter I have five fictive brothers: Glenn, Ken, Darren, Terry and Les, all more or less between the ages of thirty-five and fifty and all animal rights activists.

Glenn
Glenn Lyons is a physicist who looks like the archangel Gabriel; Scottish with long black hair, to my great joy he dedicated his PhD 'To Joan

and the Moggies'. When he was living locally, he would put up notices like 'Drive Carefully – Cats Crossing' and once sat uncomplaining on the sofa with my third Siamese, Jan, on his lap when she fell into such a deep sleep that she had a small accident. As a physics student, Glenn used to store all our placards and leaflets in his rooms, where the walls were decorated with indecipherable mathematical hieroglyphics. He was very active in the animal rights movement, as a hunt saboteur and down at the Dover docks opposing live exports. Now he lives happily with Angie together with his ageing cat Minnie, and when he got a mortgage I feared he might become respectable, but my fears were unjustified.

Ken

Ken looks like a cross between a zany stand-up comedian and a born-again monk. I think we first met at a circus demonstration. Both he and Glenn were hunt saboteurs, but I think Ken got fed up with being beaten up by hunt thugs and the police. When he came to my eightieth birthday party, he gave me a photograph of Axel, a senior member of his tabby cat club. Alas, his seven cats were decimated by a virus so he now he has just two survivors. He was one of the first animal rights people who introduced me to pet rats. One of his favourites would sit on his shoulder and nibble his sandwiches. Ken was involved for a long time with rehabilitating wild animals to Africa. He taught three Caracal cats in a sanctuary to catch birds by making paper models before taking them to live on an airport in South Africa, where they made their living keeping birds off the runway and away from landing aircraft. Before he was struck down with exhaustion fatigue, he was out most nights rescuing badgers and foxes or engaged in surveillance work. Ken is decisive, reliable and impatient with people who vacillate. I too am almost excessively reliable and punctual; on one occasion I was five minutes late to meet Ken at the café for coffee and he was so anxious he was considering ringing Addenbrookes hospital. Ken is very attractive and I've threatened to put him up for auction. Apart from being one of my dearest friends, I depend on him to restore the world to order when it gets out of hand – for instance, when the doorbell won't work or the television goes out of action – but I also depend on his judgment on the many tricky situations I land myself in.

Darren

If I wanted one word to describe Darren it would be 'steadfast'. He appeared at one of our animal rights meetings eight years ago and became an instant vegan. Since then, he and I have attended innumerable meetings and demonstrations. Solid and reassuring, it was amazing to have him as a fellow deckhand on the *Farley Mowat* with Sea Shepherd. I was not on the Antarctic expedition, but we were together during the Brazilian campaign. Subsequently Darren became Quartermaster on the *Farley Mowat*. He loves wild nature and was ecstatic as the waves broke over him and the birds wheeled around his head. He returned to England to raise money for Sea Shepherd to buy a faster ship to chase and sink the Japanese whalers, and the latest news is that he is aboard the new ship in the Antarctic.

Terry Woods

Terry is in his fifties, the oldest of my brothers. I first really got to know him at the protest camp outside Huntingdon Life Sciences. He is a safe engineer (he can pick locks!) He says that in his youth he would shoot everything in sight and was a 'normal' macho young man, a meat eater and a heavy drinker. Then on one occasion he shot a jackdaw and it did not die. He tried to wring its neck but still it did not die and suddenly he was appalled by his action and nursed the bird back to relative health. This must have been well over twenty years ago. Then for some odd psychological reason he opted to become a taxidermist, as if to make reparation for the animals he had killed. He says he was 'redeemed' at the age of twenty-eight and has since given his life to animal welfare and animal rights, becoming well respected within the movement, renowned as a teacher in schools and colleges and receiving accolades for his work. Terry makes a wonderful impression when he gives talks to schools and college students. Tough, 'macho' and well tattooed, the students are amazed to hear him expound his views on veganism. He is surprisingly sensitive to other people's state of mind. Once during our time at the camp, when I was feeling suicidal, he rang me late at night as he was concerned for my state of mind: I had decided to watch a film on television and then to take my life – thanks Terry! Now divorced, Terry is living with Kate, about twenty cats, a lurcher dog and working voluntarily at an animal sanctuary.

Les

Les is long, lean and gaunt. We first met during the campaign against Huntingdon Life Sciences. He's been a vegetarian since he was fifteen and spent his youth travelling, involved in anti-war campaigns and an anarchist punk rock group. Like Ken and Glenn, he was a hunt saboteur until it became too violent. Later he was arrested for trying to stop the Grand National. The charges were dropped and he became active on many other animal rights campaigns, as well as working with ex-model Celia Hammond rescuing and trapping stray cats in London. He is now working as a gardener and has this gentle compassion for the living world, a characteristic of all my fictive brothers.

My fictive family also includes many women friends. Although I've never been involved in the feminist movement, I have campaigned with Fran, mother of the little boy Jordan whom I described tackling the fisherman at the age of four. When we first met in Cambridge, she was demonstrating against pornography in the days before it was the burning issue it is now. I joined her at the newsagents when she and her friends were removing dirty magazines and throwing them on the floor, banging wooden spoons against empty cat food tins until we were removed by the police. Later we occupied a pornography shop, but I had an alarming time when the angry proprietor said he would call the police and accuse me of theft. Fortunately the local policeman did not believe him. Fran has always been at the forefront of anti-war campaigns and was a veteran of Greenham Common.

I am dependent on female friends and have never understood how women can get through life without such intimacy. I value Pat and Sue and others in the Gran-archist group. Then there are my 'respectable' friends, my beloved spiritual sister Nicola, and my next door neighbour Rosemary – daughter of a Methodist academic –who lives a strangely law-abiding life, working in the university and devoting every minute of her free time to the RSPCA. We have been neighbours for about fifteen years and have never had any major arguments, perhaps because we rarely communicate except in an emergency through an exchange of notes. In times of emergency, Rosemary is always there for me, appearing mysteriously by my side, for instance when burying a cat or some other difficulty.

There are other women to whom I'm deeply attached, including Fiona, who with her partner Wayne will one day inherit my house. I met her when she telephoned to ask if I could help with her little cat, who was disturbing the neighbours with her constant meowing but then came to live with me and for some reason decided to live a quieter life. My other pagan friend (Fran is the first) is Greta, the girl who locked herself underground in the Huntingdon Life Sciences campaign. She now works with Fox Rescue and as a healer.

I do have one or two friends of my own age, including the elegant Lady Lena Brown, who lives in a beautiful house with numerous rescued feral cats and has a direct line by video to her badger sets. She may not be so popular in the village, as she has chased off the hunters and others who would decimate wildlife. When the master of the local hunt rode his horses over her land, she stood in his way and he challenged her saying "Who are you?" When she told him, he doffed his cap apologetically and was never again seen on her land.

I have a few younger friends, most of whom I have known since they were thirteen. Eloise, who claims she knows more about my life than I do, acts as a wonderful memory bank; an interesting young woman with a caustic wit, destined to become an academic. After obtaining a First in her undergraduate degree, she is now well away with her PhD in Politics. She has remained faithful to her campaign against circuses and I watch her academic successes with amazement. There is also little Joe, whom I met when he, too, was thirteen and we were occupying a bank in protest. I tend to be protective of him and did not want him to get in trouble with the police. We have kept in touch over the years and I was amused recently when I was sitting in the hunt saboteur van, a tall young man turned to me and I recognised Joe. He then reversed our roles by saying, "Joan, I think you should stay in the van – it's getting a bit rough out there." Lastly, Ros, who at thirteen led her school on an anti-Iraq war demonstration, fawn-like, independent, with an irreverent attitude towards her school which she looked forward to leaving, planning a career as a paramedic but currently she is in an anarchist squat, a full-time animal rights campaigner and active in the anti-war movement.

My fictive family would not be complete without telling you about my cats. Pushkin came with me to Cambridge from London, Siamese, and the runt of her litter. She died when she was seventeen. One of her problems was that she could not travel by car at a speed greater than twenty miles an hour, which posed a difficulty if we ever had to rush to the vet. Suki-Suzanna also lived to a great age. Over the last twenty-five years, many other cats have lived with me, and now I have just seven: Wilhelmina, the beautiful Siamese; Poppy, whom I rescued from the street and is handicapped, having lost her tail through an accident. A little survivor who likes to think she is a rabbit, she cannot understand when she is rebuffed by them. If she can, she will sleep in the rabbit hutch. Patsy, Ken's favourite, is a little tortoiseshell who came from a shelter having been twice an adolescent mother. Penelope, from Cats Protection, also gets called Penny but dislikes being so diminished. Katy, a very splendid tortoiseshell, was found by a friend of mine, wandering down Newmarket Road apparently looking for her home. She came to live with me and as I was unable to trace her family she has now accepted that she is adopted, but for a time she was sad. Molly – aged sixteen, tabby and white, and a Londoner – disturbed my other felines with her terrible command of Cockney swearwords and for a time would not allow any other cat to go unchallenged up or down the stairs, which posed a problem. She now puts up with the other cats, except for Wilhelmina whom she has never believed is a real cat, which is hardly surprising. The most recent arrivals are Maisie Maple, a 17 year old jet black panther from a local sanctuary, who is stone deaf, and Freda whom I inherited when her 'human' died. She is 19, one eyed, deaf and very vocal.

Being so attached to my feline friends makes it very difficult to go away. When I went to sea on the *Farley Mowat* a friend remarked, "I hope you find a cat in every port". Fortunately, as recounted elsewhere, Captain Watson brought Itarqui on board, who became my devoted friend and still sends me emails from her home with the captain's wife.

You may think that all my friends are beautiful, brave and intelligent, and this is true as I am a born-again elitist, but I am also intensely interested in people and watch with love and interest how things develop for them.

Glenn and Millie

Ken and Bob

Darren

Terry and Ollie

Les with Toby and Teabag

97

Chapter Nineteen

Social Movements Change the Way People Think

Social Change is a violent enterprise and always has been. There has never been a successful non-violent social or political revolution in the history of humankind.

Captain Paul Watson, Sea Shepherd

We may be different from some other resistance movements. Animal rights people are certainly not composed of middle class *Guardian* readers. I know we are perceived by some members of the public as violent terrorists, attitudes hyped up by the media reflecting the opposition and fear of those most likely to be harmed by our stance, i.e. corporate business, intensive farmers, vivisectors and all those involved in making money from exploiting animals. Historically there is nothing new in the attitude of those who oppose social change. I can remember when the movement against tobacco brought out the evidence to support the connection with lung cancer. Investors in the tobacco industry agreed that sometimes it might cause lung disease, but suggested that people had the right to choose their own lifestyle – but of course, people did not have the facts on which to make their own judgment and the government did not want to lose the revenue from tobacco. Now things have changed, but unfortunately we still export tons of cigarettes to third world countries. The Suffragettes, too, were a threat – not to the economy, but to male vanity and the status quo: "A woman's place is in the home". Men feared that if women got the vote, the next thing they would want would be to go to university, rather like those who supported hunting with dogs and quite rightly feared that now that hunting with dogs is banned, at least in theory, we will start opposing fishing and shooting: too true - we do!

Most arguments against reform are based on greed and exploiting the powerless. For instance, when it was proposed that the hours worked by child chimney sweeps should be reduced from twelve to eight hours a day there was fear that the whole economy would collapse. Opponents of slavery were told that without slaves there would be financial ruin, and many people believed that black people were not fully human. These attitudes are very recent, by my standards. Looking back fifty years, I remember the colour bar in India and later in America. As a mild protest in India, I would sit in restaurants at railway sections which in theory were for Indians, i.e. non-whites. And on a ship going out to Cape Town in the 1940s black Americans were relegated to the steerage class, and I caused some outrage by talking with these men while travelling as a first class passenger. I think my sympathy may come from my poor benighted mother who used to invite tramps in for dinner. I invite our local street people in for tea and still give money to beggars. If they spend it on drugs or alcohol, that is of no concern to me – it's cold and miserable on the streets.

One of the interesting things about the animal rights movement is that it is the only social movement that is not concerned with improving the status of human beings but is intent on saving other species. Members of the animal rights movement, compassionate activists, have a clear vision of the moral value and status of all creatures and of their interdependence. I sometimes wonder if we may appear strange to 'ordinary people'. Do we carry things to extremes? I hope so. For example, when I was invaded by ants on the sideboard, Ken said "Leave them a note", so I did. But when they persisted in looking for the sugar bowl I gave them an ultimatum to move next door or else! And in their own time they left. Darwin was fascinated by the lives of ants, particularly what he perceived as their altruistic social cohesion. Again, it was my mother who told me that we should not take the life of any living creature as we cannot replace it.

Our movement is certainly classless and our age range from four to ninety-plus. There may be more women, and a higher proportion of people of retirement age because, contrary to public perception, most of us are employed or retired. A few might claim that they do not particularly like animals but are appalled by the injustice and exploitation of helpless animals in laboratories, farming, circuses, zoos, horse racing, greyhound racing and above all, perhaps, in the meat trade. The idea of eating animals and their by-products, including fish of course, is so repugnant to us that sometimes our attitude quite puts off young lovers who complain that their partner should not always wear a T-shirt inscribed *Meat Is Murder* during intimate contact. And I wrote a poem inscribed *I will not sleep with men who eat meat* – I should be so lucky at eighty nine!

Thinking of my friends in the movement, I was recently at a demonstration in Oxford against a testing laboratory. It was entirely peaceful. Talking to my contacts there, I noted that they included an economist, a retired naval officer, three teachers, five social workers, a gardener, numerous IT wizards, a contortionist called Rubber Richie, a vet, nurses, night watchmen and cleaners, as well as hundreds of new faces - the young and ardent, mothers pushing prams or granny in a wheelchair, all fired by the same passion and pity, and a profound empathy.

Chapter Twenty

Lamentations

I have seen a grievous evil under the sun

Ecclesiastes 5:13

Electrons can be in two places at once and physicists are working on making time go backwards but until they do, human beings have the privilege of growing old. I am conscious in my eighty-ninth year of being a young girl pretending to be an old lady as I struggle with my arthritic hips getting into a car, walking at a snail's pace on demonstrations, tending to be the last one at the back, gently prodded by a police horse. All this became more obvious to me after I returned from the *Farley Mowat*. I had noticed diminishing energy over the last five years of my working life, when I stopped more frequently at working men's cafes for a strong cuppa and a chance to sit down, and I was amazed on crowded London tube trains to be offered a seat – usually by a woman, frequently black. But on demonstrations I could be useful, delaying traffic, hobbling slowly across the road clutching Hilda's walking stick till told by a policeman, "You can go faster than that, Joan". I see no reason why one should come to terms with old age any more than one should overcome bereavement. Psychiatrists make ponderous statements on the way we should make our way through 'the normal grieving process'. The current jargon refers to 'closure'.

People face devastation in individual ways and the prescriptive mantra to be applied when someone or something vital is lost is at best unhelpful and at worst imposes an artificial boundary on a dynamic process. When Ken lost his beloved human partner, Alice, he was comforted by an eight-year-old who said "Why don't you dig her up, then you would have her bones to cuddle", thus showing a deep empathy. Growing old is a loss even though one does wear purple and can disregard appropriate behaviour. A cardiac consultant writing to my GP said, "This patient does not seem to know what is appropriate behaviour for a woman of her age", just because I'd asked his opinion on the advisability on embarking on a trip to the North Sea to save whales, though in the event I actually went with Sea Shepherd to Brazil. A decade ago, the stereotyping of the elderly came home to me when we were sitting around a camp fire sipping our tea and a young man passed a joint around. When it came to my turn, he reached straight accross me to the girl sitting next to me, 'Do you mind!' I said indignantly – not that cannabis is my thing, but I resented being thought of as past it.

Elderly people complain about memory loss and say they can no longer remember names but always never forget a face. This doesn't bother me much as I have always forgotten both names and faces. I have always had to be careful not to give offence when greeted 'Hello Joan, how lovely to see you' and I haven't a clue who it is. I seldom forget dates and appointments, thanks to notes under the teapot saying "telephone the vet", "beans for rabbit", "write to prisoners". Other signs of encroaching dementia are more likely due to not paying attention to what I'm doing, "You just don't look", says Ken, as I fiddle with the safety belt in the car and leave the front door keys in the door. Recently Darren remarked, "Is your doorbell meant to be upside down?" I had noticed it was not ringing. I was slightly worried recently when going through my normal bedtime routine, checking the gas cooker, turning off the lights and carrying Wilhelmina upstairs (does she need a stair lift?) I was about to pour fruit juice into the hot water bottle. But a young friend cheered me up when she told me she had put her slippers in the oven instead of the washing machine.

I look at my wrinkled skin, which is gently picked up by Wilhelmina leaving a surprising bruise, and fall asleep in my armchair encased by warm and purring cats. I feel no need to turn off the television, leaving Wilhelmina to look over her shoulder to lip read. When I complain about the minor discomforts of old age, Ken says "You're wearing out".

Are there any advantages in old age? I don't know anyone who thinks that there are, although in the animal rights movement I can exploit my age for media attention, particularly on hunger strikes and perhaps to encourage younger activists to keep going. But how can we sleep at night remembering the tattered bodies of flesh and bone in vivisection laboratories, the holocaust of the seals on the ice flows of Newfoundland and Labrador, the bored tigers in cages and zoos and the magnificent elephants made to perform absurd and degrading acts in circuses, or shackled and shut in beast wagons. Elephants weep, and I weep for them

I appreciate that human beings are in some ways privileged to live so long whereas most non-domestic animals, unless they are eking out their lives in zoos or circuses, die young. I think particularly of the cows. I have a non-vegetarian friend who claims that if we were all vegetarians we would not have the joy of seeing the animals in pasture, as though her aesthetic image were of more importance than the true fate of these animals.

The plight of cows is highlighted by Andrew Tyler in his account of 'zero grazing':

"The industry-promoted image of Daisy among the buttercups has long been bogus but now dairy farming has arrived at a critical new juncture with the arrival of the almost permanently confined battery cow. Her fate is to eke out a short existence inside large sheds, shared with hundreds of other cows. Each has a narrow metal-barred stall. They are moved two or three times a day to the automated milking unit. Some operations also have covered 'loafing' yards. It is the cow equivalent of battery hen production – a system now widely regarded as inhumane.

In general, dairy cows suffer a high level of illness and disease but in zero-grazing systems, the problems intensify… Permanently confined cows suffer from lameness, mastitis, infertility, acidosis and laminitis."

The fate of Mother Cow is particularly heart-rending as her feet hurt all the time and she's often made to walk too fast and cannot see where she puts them. Elderly people will sympathize, but they have remedies for their bunions and corns. Mother Cow with her grossly distended udders cannot walk properly. Modern cows are so large that they cannot fit into the cubicle so their feet are often in the slurry. Old people in hospital may sympathise as they are pulled about and have to go for another scan, but Mother Cow suffers routinely as antibiotics are injected into her teats. The elderly in hospital are frequently hungry, thirsty and malnourished, unable to reach the tea placed out of reach on the locker unless a kind nurse or visitor sees their plight and holds the rapidly cooling liquid to parched lips. Mother Cow, too, is also always hungry, unable to eat enough to produce the high yield of milk required of her. Even more difficult for her is having her male calves taken away (one hundred thousand a year) after twenty-four hours with their mother, usually to be shot and fed to the hunt hounds or shipped out to the cruel veal crates of Europe. The cow's female babies are also usually removed from her after twenty four hours, so she spends most of her life in grief and physical pain, and may even be pregnant when she goes for slaughter.

I have likened the suffering of elderly human beings to that of cows, but at least human beings normally live into adulthood whereas farm animals including cows have their life-spans cut grossly short. Our callous indifference to animal suffering extends to our cynical neglect of elderly human beings. Elderly people are not often put down, though many wish they could be and all old people need an advocate outside the medical profession. One often reads in obituaries that someone died 'peacefully after a long illness' but I doubt whether this is usually the case. There are only three thousand hospice beds in the country and most human beings will die without dignity in hospital, frequently frightened by the delirium brought on by morphine and the pain, miserably uncomfortable either waiting for a bedpan or left on one for ages.

There is considerable discussion now about the merits and perils of assisted suicide. I personally think we should, if at all possible, make our own decisions and plan to terminate our own lives if riddled with pain. There are situations where it may not be physically possible to do this, but usually with good planning it is. There is plenty of information about this on the Internet. I do not see why we should expect doctors or relatives to give us fatal injections sanctioned by law.

As for the poor cows, if I may continue the comparison with our own aging, we are mistaken in thinking that Hindus and others who have a special relationship with Mother Cow treat her well. Hare Krishna followers, for example, carefully tend their own cattle but outside their community drink cows' milk, as do many Buddhists and others who belong to faiths that preach compassion to all sentient beings. Cruelty to animals is endemic to all major religions, including Christianity. Similar criticisms can be made of Judaism and Islam. According to Tony Wardle, "No matter how compassionate their original teaching, Judaism and Islam have built huge bureaucracies around animal killing and meat eating and will defend it till the death so to speak – so aggressively you would think their very lives depended upon slicing open the throat of a fully conscious animal. So if it is moral judgement that you are looking for, you won't find it in the UK's major religions" (*Viva! Life*, Spring 2006).

I find this lack of animal care particularly sad as when I was in India fifty years ago cows roamed around the streets garlanded with marigolds, some without owners, eating the nutritious vegetables and sugar cane from the rubbish heaps and harbouring their strength by sitting in a sunny spot usually in the middle of the road. They may have been neglected, but suffering was not inflicted on them. Now because India is 'developed' – a word that usually means destruction – in ways that would have horrified Gandhi, the government has ordered the clearing of the city streets in Delhi, for example, not only of poor and destitute humans but also of wandering cows. In 2006, ten thousand cattle were removed from the streets and left in city 'shelters'. There they are starved of food and water till they die. Their emaciated bodies are then used for leather, fertiliser and glue. There has always been a thriving market for cow skins, with India's lower castes specialising in tanning and the leather trade. This appalling suffering is not confined to India and Indians, but somehow one feels particularly disillusioned to read about it happening in a country where the majority worship Krishna. As long ago as 1946, Gandhi told me he drank goat's milk because he knew of the exploitation of cattle. There are splendid Indian animal rights campaigners, including distinguished politicians, fighting to reform the most blatant animal abuse. Meanwhile, it would help if Asians in this country would make a stand and drink soya milk. Their beliefs are deeply embedded in feelings, and their erroneous beliefs in the nutritional value of cow's milk are hard to change.

To conclude this memoir, I believe we interfere in nature at our peril as the human race rushes in a senseless and suicidal drive to ultimate destruction. I still remain interested in the possibility of living a good life, conscious that we are all foolish beings, as the Dharmavidya says, and likely to fall about doing more harm than good some of the time. But I've reached the age when I'd quite like to retire to the forest or live in an Indian village, preferably in Bengal, with my retired buffalo and no other duties than to take him for a wallow in the pond and feed him delicious sugar cane.

Like many older people, I'm not troubled about dying. I would of course like to die on a high note, perhaps driving a tractor through Huntingdon Life Sciences or the Oxford laboratory site as a Buddhist nun suggested. However, I fear I will not die on a demonstration, which would be great publicity, but in some ghastly supermarket or shopping mall. I hope and do actually believe there is a parallel universe and that I may well be greeted with loving paws – and Hilda, of course, who will complain, "Why have you been so long?"

THREE WISHES

When I die I will go with the jaguar through the flooded forest,
Feel his spray shattered rainbow droplets in my eyes,
Share his lair, the leaves, the bark, the rank smelling vines
And lie in the hollow of his rich fur, paws enclosed.

I will swim with the dolphins,
In the caves and bays and far out to sea,
Playing with coconut shells, banana leaves, the island debris
Tossing it to the stars.

I will go with sheep in their death trucks
Taking no space, packed in their terror
Holding them close, feeling with warmth,
On their journey through hell,
To find in death at last their own kind
In the daisy scented fields of paradise
Let me be there.

Appendix 1

Report by Dr Dan Lyons

"In spring 2000, out of the blue, I received a package containing thousands of pages of photocopied documents and a CD-Rom called 'Jackpot'. The contents were stunning. The papers described one of the most hyped, yet extreme programmes of animal research in the UK in the last decade: pig-to-primate organ transplant experiments. 'Jackpot' was an apt title. This was an enormous leak of historic significance, which had emerged from a Cambridge-based biotech firm, Imutran Ltd, part of the pharmaceutical mega corporation Novartis Pharma.

The documents revealed in graphic detail the horrific fate of some five hundred higher primates – the cousins of human beings – as they were transported thousands of miles to face certain death in the experiments, conducted at the notorious Huntingdon Life Sciences' establishment. For the first time, we at Uncaged believed we could present the raw facts about animal experiments. There would be no room for spin or obfuscation – the researchers themselves told in their own words how monkeys and baboons died in fits of vomiting and diarrhoea, spasms and body tremors, seeping wounds and bloody discharges, grinding teeth and uncontrollable eye movements… or just quiet and huddled as they sickened and were 'sacrificed', to use the cold parlance of the animal labs.

We called our report and campaign "Diaries of Despair" in recognition of the harrowing fates of the primates, meticulously logged by the technicians who were, they would protest, only following orders.

But the implications of the exposé were even greater than the enormous contribution to an informed public debate that we hoped for. Among the documents was correspondence with the Home Office – the Government departments charged with enforcing the law intended to regulate experiments on animals – the Animals (Scientific Procedure) Act 1986. A growing body of evidence obtained from undercover investigations and careful analysis of public statements strongly suggested that Government protestations of 'strict regulations', 'protection of animals' welfare' and 'only absolutely necessary experiments' was no more than empty rhetoric that concealed a policy enforced entirely for the benefit of those who experimented on animals. This new evidence was the final, damning confirmation.

The shocking suffering that clearly breached official limits, private talk by the Home Office of 'rubber-stamping', Government connivance with Imutran to evade regulations, Ministerial lies and cover-ups to Parliament, the total lack of progress in the research – all these pointed to a political scandal of unique proportions. I spent months studying the documents and consulting with a scientific and a legal advisor. I remember vividly our lawyer describing the overwhelming public interest that justified our intended publication of what we knew to be highly confidential information. What we didn't realise at the time was that it would take a two-and-a-half year legal battle to prove it.

The central recommendation of the Diaries of Despair report was for the establishment of an independent judicial inquiry into the Government's dereliction of its most fundamental duty – to uphold the rule of law and reflect the wishes of Parliament and the electorate. Our focus has been on ensuring due process: an honest and fair application of the law to ensure, before permission for vivisection is granted, that the suffering that animals are likely to experience is given proper weight and, on the other hand, that the potential benefits put forward by researchers are properly scrutinised. This is the cost/benefit assessment that is supposed to be at the heart of the regulatory system.

It must be said that we don't agree that the deliberate infliction of harm on innocent individuals, whatever species they belong to, is justifiable. But whatever one's perspective on the moral status of animals and the scientific validity of animal experiments, surely everyone agrees, at the very least, that the Government should not indulge in malpractice and dishonesty.
It's that commitment to basic principles of democracy that has sustained us through an ordeal that, among other things, could have resulted in my personal bankruptcy thanks to Imutran naming me personally as a Defendant. (Ironically, that intimidating move proved their undoing as it enabled me to

obtain legal aid, albeit the longest and most difficult application that my solicitors, Bindman & Partners, had ever experienced.) Despite a perverse interim judgment from senior judge Andrew Morritt (two hobbies listed in Who's Who: shooting and fishing), and a contemptuous Home Office stonewall led by Jack Straw, the multi-billion pound drug giant has been forced to concede to the strengths of our public interest arguments – the very same arguments which irresistibly lead to a proper independent inquiry.

A further leak last autumn, this time from the Home Office, strengthens our case and reveals new depths of deceit on the part of Government officials whose overriding priority has been to protect the interests of industry and perpetuate a callous and duplicitous policy. This legal victory is a historic turning point in one of the most controversial and significant debates of modern times. The argument can now be played out on a firmer footing: primary documentation that gives an unparallel insight into the true impact of animal experiments – and the lies and political chicanery that sustains it. The Diaries of Despair affair demonstrates in unique fashion the urgent need for profound changes in our political landscape. While New Labour pays lip service to the notion of animal welfare, the truth of the matter is that the economic demands of industry always take priority over the most fundamental interests of animals. The only party that offers a serious ethical policy is the Green Party. Without a charter of animal rights, as proposed by the Greens, animals will continue to be sacrificed without mercy in the power game politics of the three main parties."

Appendix 2
Examples of animal experiments submitted by Animal Aid.

1. Cambridge: Rat heroin addicts' drug-seeking behaviour is affected when gene-altering chemicals are injected into their brains

At the Department of Experimental Psychology, University of Cambridge, rats had cannulae implanted into a region of their brains known as the 'basolateral amygdala' (BLA), which is responsible for the formation of emotional memories. They were then trained to seek heroin by means of pressing a lever, and made to become dependent on the drug via continually active heroine-filled pumps located under their skin. The rats were then subjected to heroin withdrawal, and were trained to associate this with intermittent noises, flashing lights and strong odours.

The authors showed that, in the subsequent presence of these stimuli, the rats no longer sought heroin via the lever. This suppression of heroin-seeking was, however, obliterated when the rats' BLAs had been infused with an agent that blocked the activity of a particular gene within it, prior to them associating the above stimuli with heroin withdrawal. Following the experiments, the rats were suffocated using carbon dioxide. The authors concluded that drug withdrawal memories undergo reconsolidation in the BLA region of rats' brains, which involves the activity of a particular gene

Comment:
Drug dependency is a complex phenomenon, in which issues such as personal circumstances, genetic predisposition, local culture and self-esteem all play a part. People and not rats are the only relevant 'model' for understanding why and how people become addicted and how their condition might be remedied.

Source:
Disrupting Reconsolidation of Conditioned Withdrawal Memories in the Basolateral Amygdala Reduces Suppression of Heroin Seeking in Rats. *The Journal of Neuroscience* (2006) 26 (49): 12694 -12699. Kim G. C. Hellemans et al.

2. London: Rats with a penchant for junk food give birth to similarly affected offspring

In a study funded by the Wellcome Trust, researchers at the Royal Veterinary College fed pregnant rats on a diet of biscuits, marshmallows, cheese, jam doughnuts, chocolate chip muffins, butter flapjacks, potato crisps and caramel/chocolate bars, which continued through breastfeeding until weaning. They found that pups born from those mothers ate much more 'junk food' than pups from mothers given only a 'normal' diet of rat chow - concluding that the offspring of mothers indulging in junk food are somehow pre-programmed to be partial to junk food when they're born, and that human mothers-to-be ought to be abstinent in this regard to prevent human babies from being similarly affected

Comment:
However, there is no significant evidence to suggest that the same effect is present in humans - and, of course, it is simple common sense for pregnant women to eat a healthy. balanced diet. A number of nutritionists and child-health specialists questioned the results of the study and its applicability to humans, and warned against extrapolating this data to people. All rats were killed after the experiment.

Source:
A maternal 'junk food' diet in pregnancy and lactation promotes an exacerbated taste for 'junk food' and a greater propensity for obesity in rat offspring. *British Journal of Nutrition* (2007, online) doi: 10.1017/S0007114507812037. Stephanie A. Bavola et al.

3. Kitten Experiment
Ten five-week-old kittens had the eyelids of one eye sewn together and kept closed for ten days. In five of the kittens, the sewn eye was then opened, while the healthy eye was surgically manipulated to make it squint. Fourteen days later, the kittens were anaesthetised and had part of their skulls removed in

order to expose the brain area that is responsible for vision. Behavioural and optical imaging experiments were subsequently performed.

Comment:
There is no mention in the article of whether the kittens were allowed to recover from the experiment or whether they were euthanased. The authors do not provide any clear conclusion. Instead, they explain why their study appears to contradict that of other researchers, and also why the results could differ when the experiment is performed in monkeys.

This is yet another minor variation on a category of research called 'monocular deprivation', often used to study the human condition known as amblyopia ('lazy eye'). Cats were used in this experiment even though their eyes lack a macula and fovea, two areas of critical importance in the human eye. A Harvard trained pediatric opthalmologist commented on this type of research in 1990 in an affadavit (next column) presented in an Israeli court of law. This document, together with several other sworn statements made by eye specialists, all concurred on the lack of applicability of these experiments to the human condition.

'I do not believe that straining to find out new ways of depriving cats of visual input has added, or will add, to our knowledge about the connections of the eye to the visual cortex in cats... even if it adds a little to our knowledge of visual connections in cats, the applicability of this knowledge to human amblyopia is essentially nil. Clinical research, done with children who are actually suffering from amblyopia, would seem to be the only way to find out more about how to treat this important condition which affects about two per cent of the population.' Affidavit by Petersen MD. The Children's Hospital, Boston USA

Source:
Correlated binocular activity guides recovery from monocular deprivation. *Nature* 2002: Vol. 416: 430-433. Kind P, Mitchell D, Ahmed B, Blakemore C, Bonhoeffer T, Sengplel F. University laboratory of physiology, Parks Road. Oxford.

Funding:
Wellcome Trust. Medical Research Council (UK), Max-Planck-Gesellschaft, Canadian Institutes of Health Research, Oxford McDonnell Centre for Cognitive Neuroscience

4. University College London: 1983 monkey eye experiments repeated in 2005

Researchers at the Wellcome Laboratory of Neurobiology at the University College, London, experimented on monkeys to identify exactly which brain cells recognise colour shades. Six male macaques were used. The tests were conducted on four anaesthetised, and two conscious animals.

Two monkeys were trained to sit in a 'primate chair' - an apparatus that severely restricts body movement. Under anaesthesia, a recording device was implanted into their skulls, using stainless steel screws and dental cement. After regaining consciousness, they were immobilised in the chair and trained to stare at a point on a screen in front of them, whose background changed colour.

Similar experiments were conducted in the four anaesthetised monkeys, whose eyes could still register and transmit light waves. All six animals were killed and their brains examined.

Comment:
The authors admitted that equivalent knowledge of cell function was obtained during monkey experiments conducted in 1983.

Source:
Kusunoki M, Moutoussis K, Zeki S. *J Neurophysiol* 2006; 95:3047-3059. 'Effect of background colours on the tuning of colour-sensitive cells in monkey area V4.'

Funding:
Wellcome Trust.

5. Chemical burns in pigs
Scientists in the Biomedical Sciences Department at the Ministry of Defence, Porton Down, used pigs to test the effects of a well-known corrosive chemical agent. Three Large White pigs were anaesthetised and then exposed to the effects of Lewisite. This chemical, known since 1918, is extremely toxic and can produce full-thickness (i.e. third-degree) burns when applied to the skin. Its effects have already been well documented in the scientific literature.

After exposure to the chemical, which produced severe skin blistering, the test animals were allowed to recover from the anaesthetic. Twenty-four hours later, all three pigs were killed by lethal injection, and tissue samples taken.

The researchers concluded that the test results were consistent with those reported by other scientists in 1994, 1989 and 2002. It was also concluded that the present study confirmed the use of the Large White breed of pig as an 'appropriate model' for pursuing further such studies.

Source:
Examination of Changes in Connective Tissue Macromolecular Components of Large White Pig Skin Following Application of Lewisite Vapour. Lindsay CD, Hambrook JL, Brown RF, Platt JC, Knight R, Rice P Biomedical Sciences Department, Dstl Porton Down. Salisbury, Wiltshire) *Journal of Applied Toxicology* 2004;24:37-46.

Resources

Readers may like to contact national groups for further information. This list is only a selection from hundreds of societies that campaign for animals.

Animal Aid
(campaign against all animal abuse)
The Old Chapel, Bradford Street
Tonbridge, Kent, TN9 1AW
01732 364546 www.animalaid.org.uk/

The Captive Animals' Protection Society
(campaign against circuses that use performing animals, and expose the cruelty imposed on animals in zoos)
PO Box 4186
Manchester, M60 3ZA
0845 330 3911 www.captiveanimals.org/

Coalition to Abolish the Fur Trade
(campaigns against the fur trade)
PO Box 38
Manchester, M60 1NX
0845 330 7955 www.caft.org.uk/

International Primate Protection League
(defends all monkeys and apes, wild or captive, and supports sanctuaries world wide)
Gilmore House, 166 Gilmore Road
London, SE13 5AE
020 8297 2129 www.ippl-uk.org/

League Against Cruel Sports
(campaigns against so called "sports"; hunting, shooting and fishing)
New Sparling House
Holloway Hill, Godalming
Surrey, GU7 1QZ
01483 524 250 www.league.org.ok/

People for the Ethical Treatment of Animals
(mounts highly theatrical and effective campaigns against cruelty to animals worldwide)
PO Box 36668
London. SE1 1WA
020 7357 9229 www.peta.org.uk/

Sea Shepherd Conservation Society
(mounts unrelenting campaigns at sea to save whales and other creatures in the oceans)
www.seashepherd.org

Uncaged Campaigns
(very active and effective anti-vivisection campaigns, politically and academically focussed)
5th Floor
Alliance House, 9 Leopold Street
Sheffield, S1 2GY
0114 272 2220 www.uncaged.co.uk/

Viva! Vegetarians International Voice for Animals
(politically active and informative campaigning group promoting cruelty free living)
8 York Court
Wilder Street, Bristol, BS2 8QH
0117 944 1000 www.viva.org.uk/

References

There is now a massive literature on animal rights and welfare, political, philosophical, religious, medical, historical etc, so I have taken a minimalist approach to recommended reading!

The Silent Ark by Juliet Gellatley
One of the most chilling accounts of the meat industry written by the Director of Viva! Available from Viva!

When Elephants Weep by Jeff Masson
One of the earlier and heart breaking accounts of the emotional lives of animals, revealing their complexity. Available from Animal Aid

The Face on your Plate 2008 also by Jeff Masson
This shows how food affects our moral selves, our health and our planet.

Sacred Cows and Golden Geese: The Human Cost of Experiments on Animals by Ray and Jean Greek
Excellent account of the misconceptions relating to animal experiments and the alternatives.

From Dusk 'til Dawn by Keith Mann
Massive volume; a well researched history of the animal liberation movement, with an introduction by Benjamin Zephaniah.
Available from Viva